Michalis Vazirgiannis

Interactive Multimedia Documents

Modeling, Authoring, and Implementation Experiences

 Springer

Series Editors

Gerhard Goos, Karlsruhe University, Germany
Juris Hartmanis, Cornell University, NY, USA
Jan van Leeuwen, Utrecht University, The Netherlands

Author

Michalis Vazirgiannis
Athens University of Economics and Business
Department of Informatics
76 Patision Street, GR-10434 Athens, Greece
E-mail: mvazirg@aueb.gr

Cataloging-in-Publication data applied for

Die Deutsche Bibliothek - CIP-Einheitsaufnahme

Vazirgiannis, Michalis:
Interactive multimedia documents : modeling. authoring, and
implementation experiences / Michalis Vazirgiannis. - Berlin ;
Heidelberg ; New York ; Barcelona ; Hong Kong ; London ; Milan ;
Paris ; Singapore ; Tokyo : Springer, 1999
    (Lecture notes in computer science ; Vol. 1564)
    ISBN 3-540-66711-3

CR Subject Classification (1998): H.5, H.3, H.4, I.7

ISSN 0302-9743
ISBN 3-540-66711-3 Springer-Verlag Berlin Heidelberg New York

© Springer-Verlag Berlin Heidelberg 1999
Printed in Germany

Typesetting: Camera-ready by author
SPIN: 10702955   06/3142 – 5 4 3 2 1 0   Printed on acid-free paper

Preface

The need for multimedia information systems is growing rapidly in a variety of fields including business, manufacturing, education, CAD, CAE, medicine etc. Due to the diverse nature of multimedia data, systems designed to store, transport, display, and manage such data must have considerably more functionality and capability than conventional information management systems. Multimedia applications can be very complex as regards the number of objects involved, their transformations in the scope of an application, and the relationships among them. These features become even more salient with the advent and wide usage of the WWW as the main medium for information dissemination.

The issue of modeling, authoring, and presenting multimedia documents has attracted significant research and industrial efforts in the last years. In this book we present an integrated framework for Interactive Multimedia Documents (IMDs). We cover most of the stages of the life cycle of an IMD: *data modeling, authoring, verification and querying, execution and rendering.* The basis of the framework is a model for IMDs that widely covers the issue of interaction and spatiotemporal composition. According to the model, an IMD is defined in terms of *actors, events,* and *scenario tuples.* The actors (video, sound, image, text, and buttons) represent the participating media objects and their spatiotemporal transformations to align to the presentation requirements. The events are the interaction primitives and they may be atomic or complex. They are generated by user actions, actors' state changes, or by the system. The basic constituent of an IMD is the scenario, namely a set of scenario tuples. A tuple is a fundamental entity of functionality in the scenario conveying information about the event(s) that start (or stop) a set of synchronized media presentations.

Based on this IMD model we develop an *authoring* methodology, clearly identifying the stages of interaction and spatiotemporal presentation specification. During the authoring process, it is vital to provide the author with *verification* facilities to review the document design and thus avoid errors and improve the design quality. The verification has to deal with the temporal and spatial dependencies and constraints of the document. We propose a methodology for verification of the spatiotemporal content of an IMD. A related issue is the ability of an author to query an IMD as regards the spatiotemporal dependencies that are inherent to it. There the requirement for efficiency is apparent. We have worked on a spatiotemporal indexing scheme that efficiently processes queries with intensive spatiotemporal content.

The result of IMD specification under this approach is a declarative script, which has to be executed whenever an IMD session is initiated. The execution (*rendering*) of an

IMD may be a complicated task due to the multitude of events occurring and the potentially large sets of different presentation options.

We developed two approaches for IMD rendering, one based on a single-thread approach and another generic multi-threaded architecture that detects and evaluates events that occur in the presentation context and triggers the appropriate synchronized presentation actions. Both schemes are implemented.

Book Overview

The book is organized in chapters, each one describing one of the aforementioned issues.

In the *first* chapter, the issue of multimedia document modeling is addressed. Moreover, a review of the research efforts aiming at modeling the various aspects of multimedia documents is provided as well as a substantial presentation of current document standards (HYTIME, MHEG, and SMIL).

In chapter *two*, the integrated IMD model is presented. The modeling approach takes into account the various aspects of a multimedia database and applications. Namely: multimedia transformations, composition of media objects in space and time, events modeling, scenario definition. Indeed, an interactive multimedia application includes media objects modified accordingly and presented according to a predefined spatiotemporal sequence or according to some interaction. The participating media objects are rarely used as they are. In most cases parts of them (cropping procedure takes place) are transformed (spatially and/or temporally) according to the authors needs. The next stage is the definition of the application functionality. We distinguish between two types of functionality: the pre-orchestrated (i.e. the spatiotemporal presentation of the participating objects is predefined) and the interactive one (i.e. the flow of the application is dependent on the interaction actions that will occur). As for the pre-orchestrated case, the spatiotemporal composition specifications have to be defined, where as for the interactive one the events that will trigger the corresponding action have to be defined. The two aforementioned procedures will produce the overall application scenario and this has to be stored in the appropriate database.

In chapter *three*, we present the authoring methodology that results from the IMD model. The authoring procedure is carried out in three consecutive phases corresponding to the basic modeling primitives: i. selection and transformation of the media objects to participate; ii. definition of the events (atomic and complex) that the IMD session will consume; the author defines the atomic events that the current IMD will exploit for the scenario; iii. specification of the IMD scenario in terms of scenario tuples.

In chapter *four*, we present the verification tools and methodologies that are available in the context of our framework. The tools may be used both for the *prototyping* and the *verification* of multimedia presentations or spatiotemporal compositions in general. Emphasis is on the flexible definition of spatial and temporal relationships of the participating entities. The *verification* procedures are supported by multiple tools allowing designers to preview their applications, in various ways: *spatial layouts* of the application window, *temporal layout* of the application, indicating the temporal duration and relationships among the participating objects and *animation (rendering)* of the application.

In chapter *five*, we present a generic framework for transformation of the IMD declarative script to an algorithmic form, in order to obtain an executable form of the document. The declarative IMD script resulting from the authoring process, is translated into a set of procedures corresponding to the constituents of the scenario, namely: the events and the scenario tuples (including the synchronized presentation actions). The result of this process is a set of procedures specific to the IMD concerned. This set of procedures is integrated in a predefined IMD template, and the result is the specific algorithmic form of the IMD document.

In chapter *six*, we address the issue of rendering an IMD. Rendering is the process of enforcing the presentation specifications of the IMD scenario, i.e. when, where, for how long, and under what transformations each media object will be presented. Here, we present two implemented designs we have carried out. A single threaded generic one and a multithreaded one appropriate for the latest technological demands arising from the WWW. Both schemes carry out the following tasks: i. detect events generated by the system, the user, or the actors and subsequently evaluate these events against the start/stop event expressions of each scenario tuple; ii. activate the appropriate tuples asynchronously and perform synchronized presentation actions according to the scenario tuples' specifications; iii. handle exceptions.

In chapter *seven*, we present a scheme for managing IMDs that involve a large number of interrelated objects. We propose an indexing scheme based on spatial indexing techniques. Thus fast retrieval of queries regarding spatiotemporal queries is feasible. Moreover spatial or temporal application layouts may be obtained.

Finally, in the appendices there is an extended example application as it is represented through the model proposed in previous chapters (Appendix A) and the formal definition of the model in terms of BNF grammar (Appendix B).

Acknowledgements

The procedure for developing ideas, making them concrete, verifying, and communicating them to the research community is a long and arduous procedure. During this procedure I was not alone. There were people (friends and colleagues) whose contributions I would like to acknowledge.

First, I want to thank the following colleagues who contributed with their implementation skills to the development of the concepts into running prototypes: Y. Stamati, M. Trafalis, D. Tsirikos, Markousis, T. Mouroulis, and Y. Politis (in chronological order).

Also I would like to thank D. Tsirikos, T. Markousis, and I. Mirbel for their kind effort in reviewing preliminary versions of parts of the book and contributing their comments, corrections, and insight.

I should also mention my co-authors in the publication history that served as the basis for this book: C. Mourlas, M. Hatzopoulos, Y. Theodoridis, S. Boll, and Y. Stavrakas (again in chronological order).

The contribution of Prof. T. Sellis to my evolution in the research domain, after my Ph.D., has been critical. I am grateful to him for offering me the friendly environment and the resources of his laboratory and for his manifold support in the various aspects of what we call research work.

Also I would like to acknowledge the support and contribution of Dr. T. Rakow for giving me the chance to work in GMD/IPSI and also for his contribution to the initiation of this work.

I am grateful to my parents (Ignatios and Angela) for their long term and no-matter-what support so far. They both have devoted to me more resources than I could expect.

Finally, I have to acknowledge Victoria's support, patience, and love throughout this effort.

Table of Contents

1.   Background

1.1   Introduction

Multimedia applications are gaining importance in the software industry due to their impact on various user communities. An important part of a multimedia application is the scenario, which describes the flow of the application in spatial and temporal domains as well as handling application and system events. Current authoring systems do not provide models and tools for complete representation of complex scenario description.

The need for multimedia information systems grows rapidly in a variety of fields including business, manufacturing, education, CAD, CAE, medicine etc. Due to the diverse nature of multimedia data, systems designed to store, transport display and in general, manage such data must have considerably more functionality and capability than conventional information management systems.

Information providers have a strong interest in creating multimedia presentations, such as electronic books enhanced by audio annotations or short video clips or dynamic WWW pages. Computer companies and major publishers created many joint ventures to get actively involved in this market. But it remains unclear in what document architecture an author should create a document for maximum portability. No single system has penetrated the world market and established a de facto standard. For example, a multimedia book would have to include several video formats, such as MPEG, and Apple's QuickTime, to reach a mass market. This is inconvenient and expensive for the producer.

Requirements for the concept of Multimedia document thus arise. There are several research models and international standards corresponding to this need (eg. HYTIME, MHEG, SMIL). Essentially a multimedia document is the orchestrated (composed) presentation of media objects (text, audio, video, animation, etc.) in the spatial and temporal domain taking also in account the interaction that may occur and thus modify the flow of this orchestration.

An Interactive Multimedia Document (IMD) involves a variety of individual multimedia objects presented according to a set of specifications called the IMD scenario. The multimedia objects that participate in the IMD are transformed, either spatially or temporally, in order to be presented according to author's requirements. Moreover, the author has to define the spatial and temporal order of objects within the document context and the relationships among them. Finally, the way that the user will interact with the presentation session as well as the way that the application will treat application or system events, has to be defined. The related application domains are quite challenging and demanding. Among others, these can be: interactive TV, digital movies, virtual reality applications and WWW pages with interactive multimedia content. Indeed, recently the WWW arises as the main information dissemination medium. As it is apparent, multimedia content is of vital importance and it is expected that the features and requirements of the WWW will affect the design of IMDs. There is already a considerable research community working on complex documents architectures potting emphasis on IMDs (e.g. The upcoming standard SMIL).

To support complex IMDs, a system that offers both a suitable high-level modeling of IMDs and interactive multimedia presentation capabilities is needed. The modeling should comprise the spatial and temporal composition of the participating media, the definition of interaction between the user and the IMD, the specification of media synchronization and the presentation quality. An interactive multimedia presentation should cover the correct reproduction of the pre-orchestrated and interactive multimedia scenarios, synchronization enforcement, the observation of presentation quality as well as a fast response to user interactions. The trend in multimedia applications not only points the way to complex multimedia scenarios and to interactivity but also to multi-user environments. Therefore, the concepts needed to support IMDs should be applicable not only to single-user but also to multi-user environment.

1.2   Basic Concepts

An IMD involves a variety of individual multimedia objects presented according to a set of specifications called the IMD scenario. The multimedia objects that participate in the IMD are transformed, either spatially or temporally, in order to be presented according to author's requirements. Moreover, the author has to define the spatial and temporal order of objects within the document context and the relationships among them. Finally, the way that the user will interact with the presentation session as well as the way that the application will treat application or system events, has to be defined. The related application domains are quite challenging and demanding. Among others, these can be interactive TV, digital movies, and virtual reality applications. In the framework of IMDs we consider the following as cornerstone concepts:

- Events: they are the fundamental means of interaction in the context of the IMD and are raised by user actions, by objects participating in the IMD or by the system. They may be simple (i.e. not decomposable in the IMD context) or complex, and have attached their spatiotemporal signature (i.e. the space and the time they occurred). For more details refer to [VB97].

- Spatiotemporal Composition: it is an essential part of an IMD and represents the spatial and temporal ordering of media objects in the corresponding domain. At this point, the issue of spatial and temporal relationships among the objects is critical [VTS98].

- Scenario: it stands for the integrated behavioral contents of the IMD, i.e. what kind of events the IMD will consume and what presentation actions will be triggered as a result. In our approach a scenario consists of a set of self-standing functional units (scenario tuples) that include: triggering events (for start and stop), presentation actions (in terms of spatiotemporal compositions) to be carried out in the context of the scenario tuple, and related synchronization events (i.e. events that get triggered when a scenario tuple starts or stops).

- Scenario Rendering: it is the process of defining an execution plan for the IMD scenario, i.e. when, where, for how long and under what transformations each media object will be presented. This task is rather straightforward in "pre-orchestrated" applications [KE96], while in the case of IMDs with rich interaction it becomes more complicated.

The IMD modeling covers widely the issue of interactive scenaria and their constituents: events and spatiotemporal composition of presentation actions. According to the model an IDM is defined in terms of *actors*, *events* and *scenario tuples*. The actors (video, sound, image, text, and buttons) represent the media objects participating and their spatiotemporal transformations [V96]. The events are the interaction primitives and they may be atomic or complex. They are generated by user actions, actors' state changes or by the system. The basic constituent of an IMD is the scenario, namely a set of scenario tuples. A tuple is a fundamental entity of functionality in the scenario conveying information about the event(s) that start (or stop) a set of synchronized media presentations (called *instruction streams* in our model). Instruction streams are expressions that involve Temporal Access Control (TAC) actions such as start, stop, pause, resume and others, on actors with the use of vacant temporal intervals in between. In [Vaz97-2] a set of operators has been defined for the TAC actions and for the corresponding events. Thus, the expression (A>3B>0C!) is interpreted as "start A, after 3 seconds start B and immediately after (0 seconds) stop C".

The result of IMD specification under this approach is a declarative script. As mentioned before the rendering of an IMD scenario may be a complicated issue regarding the multitude of occurring events and the potentially large sets of instruction streams.

The rendering of the scenario is based on a generic multi-threaded architecture that detects and evaluates events that occur in the presentation context and triggers the appropriate synchronized presentation actions. The rendering scheme has been implemented in a client-server system based on Java. The server provides the IMD, while the media objects reside in any http server. The client, in charge of rendering the IMD scenario, retrieves the scenario from the server and requests the appropriate media from the corresponding http servers. The client design covers widely the issue of interaction with external and internal entities in terms of simple and complex events. The system detects and evaluates the occurring events and triggers the appropriate presentation actions. Furthermore, it maintains the high-level spatial and temporal synchronization requirements of the application according to the IMD scenario. The whole framework has been implemented in Java using the RMI (Remote Method Invocation) client-server communication protocol and the JMF (Java Media Framework) for handling multimedia objects. The system presents a promising approach for distributed interactive multimedia on the Internet and Intranets.

In order to support complex IMDs, a system that offers both a suitable high-level modeling of IMDs and interactive multimedia presentation capabilities is needed. The modeling should comprise the spatial and temporal composition of the participating media, the definition of interaction between the user and the IMD, the specification of media synchronization and the Quality of Presentation (QoP). An interactive multimedia presentation should deal with the correct reproduction of the pre-orchestrated and interactive multimedia scenaria, synchronization enforcement, observation of QoP as well as a fast response to user interactions. The trend in multimedia applications not only points the way to complex multimedia scenaria and to interactivity, but also to multi-user environments. Therefore, the concepts needed to support IMDs should be applicable not only to single-user, but also to multi-user environments.

There are many approaches to model pre-orchestrated multimedia scenaria [SKD96, WRW95, WWR95, ISO93, LG93, and ISO92]. The proposed models are mainly concerned with temporal aspects and synchronization. The support of user interaction of these models, however, is often lacking or unsatisfactory. The modeling of interactions is more complex than it may appear at first sight and certainly goes beyond 'button clicks'. In the multimedia literature, interaction is hardly addressed as a research issue. Moreover, the few approaches mentioned above that take into account interaction [SKD96, WRW95, WWR95, ISO93] are very limited, since they refer mostly to simple choices, jumps, selections and temporal control actions (start, stop, pause, resume etc.) offered to the user by means of buttons, menus and sliders.

We claim that modeling of IMDs should give more emphasis to the interactive parts of such an application. In principle, the modeling of interaction should cover all the procedures that somehow involve the machine and the user. Such procedures, apart from button manipulations, should include scrolling actions, drag and drop actions, and temporal access control actions for multimedia objects. Moreover, interaction is not limited to the reactions between the user and the computer, but can take place also between entities within the computer. For instance, objects that participate in an IMD interact spatially and/or temporally with each other, e.g., if two moving images meet across the screen. Also, resources or devices produce messages/signals that may trigger actions in the context of the IMD, e.g., if no audio device is available the equivalent text representation is displayed. When presenting multimedia scenaria, all occurring interactions must be sensed and reacted to adequately as fast as possible.

Operations on multimedia objects imply actions that modify the spatial or temporal dimensions of these objects. *Actions* describe parts of the temporal and spatial course of an IMD in contrast to *interactions* that trigger the course of an IMD. Actions can be either fundamental or composite. A fundamental (or atomic) action is, e.g., „start a video", „present or hide an image", etc. Composite actions are composed of atomic actions in the spatial and the temporal dimensions, according to a set of appropriate operators. For instance: "start video clip A, *and* 3 seconds after that, start audio clip B". In our approach we make use of this action notion, which is defined in more detail in [VTS96, VH93], in order to allow the modeling of multimedia applications to cover complex interactions.

One of the important aspects in the modeling of IMDs is the spatiotemporal composition to relate multiple media in the temporal and spatial dimensions. There are several approaches to model the temporal aspects of IMDs [LG93, WR94, BZ93, and H92], while the spatial aspects are rather under-addressed in the literature. Some of the interesting efforts in this area are [VTS96, IDG94].

The scenario of an IMD refers to the temporal/spatial ordering of the actors in the context of the IMD. In the following section we discuss the spatial / temporal aspects of IMDs.

1.3   Temporal Aspects of IMDs

In order to model the temporal aspects of an IMD, we consider a suitable representation of time. A unique point in time is denoted by a *temporal instance*, which is of zero length. A set of temporal instances is completely ordered. For any two temporal instances one of the temporal relationships before (<), after (>), or equals (=) holds. This *point-based time model* is a simple representation of time with a small number of temporal relationships. A *temporal interval* is the difference between two temporal instances. In the *interval-based time model* for any two temporal intervals one out of 13 temporal relationships holds, as outlined in [A83]. The point-based model and the interval-based model are equivalent in so far as each temporal interval [a, b] is delimited by two temporal instances, namely the start point a and the end point b of the time interval for which the temporal relationship a < b holds. For example, an interval relation I_1 *before* I_2 with $I_1 = [t_{11}, t_{12}]$ and $I_2 = [t_{21}, t_{22}]$ can be described in the point-based model by the four temporal instances $t_{11}, t_{12}, t_{21}, t_{22}$ that delimit the two intervals and the three point relationships $t11 < t_{12}$ and $t_{21} < t_{22}$ and $t_{12} < t_{21}$.

In order to make the media objects participating in an IMD scenario perceptible, they must be presented for a certain period of time, i.e., for a temporal interval. Therefore, the temporal course of a multimedia scenario corresponds to the appropriate temporal intervals, each representing the duration of presentation of a single media object. Modelling of time with intervals, however, may not be sufficient when „something happens" at an indefinite point in time during a presentation, e.g., to interactions. An interaction element such as a button might have a start point, but no definite temporal end, as the presentation of the button may end with the selection of the button by a user. Therefore, we think that in the definition phase it is sufficient to identify only these temporal instances when „something happens" in an IMD. For instance, the start of the presentation of a video, illustrated in Figure 1.1, is identified by the temporal instance t_1. This temporal instance is related to the *event* e_1 that indicates the starting point of the video presentation at t_1. An event such as e_1 is the occurrence of an action that can be recognised by a user or a process at t_1. In the example in Figure 1.1. The semantics of e_1 is: 'Start of Video x'. The temporal instance of the end of the video presentation, however, can be uncertain if it is defined to stop if a user presses a certain button. That is, event e_2, 'Video x stopped' has no temporal instance assigned to it until the actual user interaction occurs at t_2 or the video presentation simply ends.

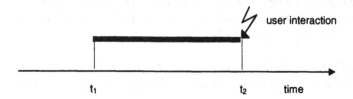

Figure 1.1. The presentation interval of a video and the associated temporal instances and events.

Although, in the context of an IMD there may be a multitude of occurring events, we might only be interested in some of them. Therefore, we propose that an event should be considered only if the IMD cares about the specific event. The temporal duration of an event is zero, as it is related to a temporal instance.

1.4   Spatial Aspects of an IMD

All visual multimedia objects (for instance image, text and video) incorporate spatial features. Thus, it is important to model the spatial semantics of an IMD. These semantics may be classified in the following categories:

- *Spatial Composition*, which refers to the representation of positions in space and the spatial relationships among participating media objects.

- *Motion*, which is an important characteristic in the context of an IMD and involves the absolute and/or relative motion of one or more media objects.

- *Spatial Events*, that are produced from actions that concern spatial relationships and/or motion. For instance, if two media objects spatially meet, an event is produced. Another example is the set of events that is generated by an object's continuous motion (still, in motion, accelerating, actual position etc.). These events may be of interest to the IMD scenario so as to trigger other actions.

A notion that we introduce in this context is the *spatial instance*, which refers to the spatial coordinates of a rectangle bounding an area of interest (x_1, y_1, x_2, y_2) relative to the origin of an IMD window. In this notation (x_1, y_1) represent the upper left corner of the rectangle and (x_2, y_2) the lower right corner.

1.5   Multimedia Document Models

In this subsection we review Multimedia synchronization modeling approaches and Multimedia document standards regarding the interaction support they provide.

In [IDG94] a model for spatiotemporal multimedia presentations is presented. The temporal composition is handled in terms of Allen relationships, whereas spatial aspects are treated in terms of a set of operators for binary and unary operations. The model lacks of the following features: there is no indication of the temporal causal relationships (i.e., what are the semantics of the temporal relationships between the intervals corresponding to multimedia objects). The spatial synchronization essentially addresses only two topological relationships: overlap and meet, giving no representation means of the directional relationships between the objects (i.e. Object A is to the right of object B) and the distance information (i.e. object A is 10 cm away from object B). The modeling formalism is oriented towards execution and rendering of the application, rather than for authoring.

In [H96] a synchronization model is presented. This model covers many aspects of multimedia synchronization such as incomplete timing, hierarchical synchronization; complex graph type of presentation structure with optional paths, presentation time prediction and event based synchronization. As regards the events, they are considered merely as presentations constrained by unpredictable temporal intervals. There is no notion of the event semantics and also no notion of composition scheme.

In [SKD96] a presentation synchronization model is presented. Important concepts introduced and manipulated by the model are the object states (Idle, ready, In-process, finished, complete). Although events are not explicitly presented, user interactions are treated. There are two categories of interaction envisaged: buttons and user skips (forward, backward).

As mentioned in [BS96], event based representation of a multimedia scenario is one of the four categories for modeling a multimedia presentation. There it is mentioned that events are modeled in HyTime and HyperODA. Events in HyTime are defined as presentations of media objects along with its playout specifications and its FCS coordinates. As regards HyperODA, events are instantaneous happenings mainly corresponding to start and end of media objects or timers. All these approaches suffer from poor semantics conveyed by the events and moreover they do not provide any scheme for composition and consumption architectures.

As regards rendering, related work has been published in [KE96]. Although it copes with multimedia objects, it models a smaller part of the IMDs that relate to the multimedia documents and not to multimedia applications. Thus, taking for granted that the document will be based on textual resources, the model tries to make an interactive multimedia "book" containing some form of multimedia objects like images, sound and video. The book is divided in chapters and the screen layout is similar to the one of word processors, along with their temporal information. The temporal relationships are taken into account, but not the spatial ones since it is assumed that they are solved depending on the text flow on the page.

There have been some research efforts on the issue of scenario verification and integrity. In [CO96], a synchronization model for the formal description of multimedia documents is presented, while in [BZ95] an approach for automatic generation of consistent presentation schedules is presented. In [CO96], the user formalization is automatically translated into a RT-LOTOS formal specification, allowing a verification of a multimedia document aiming to identify potential temporal inconsistencies. Multimedia documents are described through a hierarchical model, and incomplete timing is allowed. The user-interaction can also be represented and a media object can be expressed as one logical unit without avoiding however to refer to parts of it. A set of synchronization patterns are given, and formal semantics, in addition to a verification technique, are provided. In the proposed hierarchical model, start and end events are mandatory, while external and internal events are optional. The synchronization is done through the names of the events, or through explicit scripting. A presentation library provides monolithic and stream media objects. A constraint library is also provided. Constraints deal with temporal equalities (simultaneous events, precedence of a given event on another one, within a given temporal interval). Constraints also deal with temporal inequalities as precedence of an event to another, within an unspecified amount of time, limited by a minimum and maximum length. Constraints based on interval relationships(before, while, overlaps, ...) and termination (Wait Latest, Wait Earliest, Wait Master) are also given.

In [BZ95], a temporal constraint satisfaction algorithm is presented. The algorithm generates consistent schedules, according to acceptable durations that the author defines. The systems covers both pre-orchestrated specifications and interactive ones. The algorithm has two phases and a compile time scheduler can smooth predictable temporal inconsistencies in order to produce duration of desired/necessary duration, on the contrary of our approach where durations are not smoothed. This approach has not a clearly defined temporal composition model. Moreover the interaction supported is simple user events while in our approach we support composite events for internal and external interaction. In addition, in our approach we introduce the aspect of TAC action sequence consistency related to an object temporal state.

In [PR94] an approach is presented that addresses the key issue of providing flexible multimedia presentation with user participation and suggests synchronization models which can specify the user participation during the presentation. A Dynamic Timed Petri Nets structure is proposed to can model pre-emptions and modifications to the temp oral characteristics of the net. This structure can be adopted by the OCPN to facilitate modeling of multimedia synchronization characteristics with dynamic user participation. The authors claim that the suggested enhancements for the Dynamic Timed Petri Nets satisfy all the properties of the Petri nets theory and use the suggested enhancements to model typical scenarios in a multimedia presentation with user inputs. This effort compares as follows to the one we present in this paper:

- it has a sound theoretical background from the Petri nets theory that has been used often to model temporal synchronization of multimedia objects.

- the interaction space is different to the interaction we handle in our model. In that paper the interaction refers to the ability of the user to react with the presentation as one single object and to change global features of the presentation such as duration. Also the user can apply the well known temporal access action to the presentation such as start, pause, stop etc.

- the sequence of media objects is generally fixed (with the exception of skipping the remaining time of it) unlikely to our approach. There is no provision for interactions with the objects that participate in he presentation.

In [LK95] a framework for checking the temporal consistency of a composition of media objects is provided. The temporal composition is defined in terms of directed acyclic graphs where the nodes are objects and the edges represent temporal relations. The concepts of qualitative and quantitative inconsistency is introduced, The former one is related to the incompatibility of a set of temporal relations while the latter to the ones arising from the errors that occur due to the specific durations of media objects. The major features of the approach proposed in this paper are the following:

- the interactions are not treated explicitly, while in our case interaction and moreover complex one is the center of the design

- the temporal composition model covers the temporal relations among media objects presentation while we represent relationships using the events that are generated by the TAC actions.

1.6   Multimedia Document Standards

In this section we present three multimedia document standards: MHEG [ISO93], HyTime [ISO92] and SMIL[SML98]. They all aim at representing the structure and content of a multimedia document having a different background and origin while putting emphasis in different aspects. For instance SMIL is the upcoming standard for interactive presentations that are presented through WWW pages. On the other hand MHEG contributes in the transferability of the IMDs and allows for user interaction between the selection of one or more choices out of some user-defined alternatives.

1.6.1   Multimedia and Hypermedia Information Coding Experts Group (M H E G)

The MHEG standard aims at producing IMDs that will be transferable over various platforms, allowing an author to produce his/her work in one universally acceptable format. It also has advantages for the hardware and software suppliers. They are able to concentrate on producing the one standard MHEG engine rather than an engine for every presentation standard that is available.

The International Organization for Standardization (ISO) is developing MHEG (Multimedia and Hypermedia Information Coding Experts Group), a standard for what they call a "system independent encoding of the structure of information used for storing, exchanging, and executing multimedia presentations". MHEG is an acronym for Multimedia and Hypermedia Experts Group. This group develops within ISO (the International Standards Organization) several standards, which deal with the coded representation of Multimedia and Hypermedia Information. The main task of the group is to create a standard method of storage, exchange and display of multimedia presentations.

The JPEG and MPEG standards both describe the content of information objects only whereas they cannot describe the interrelationships between the different pieces of a multimedia presentation. The successful JPEG and MPEG standards for digital image and motion picture compression created by the same organization were all very well-defined scientific problems. However interactive multimedia exists in a completely different realm from media compression. The definition and standardization of such structure information is the purpose of the MHEG. In addition to just replaying existing multimedia data MHEG also defines some types of its own. e.g. an MHEG compliant system is able to overlay titles onto video scenes. It is also able to display menus and buttons to allow the user to make choices. The main components of the MHEG mode are the content data, behavior, user interaction, and composition.

User interaction issues consist of only two primitives: selection and modification. It seems premature to formulate a standard for multimedia productions when various aspects of the field, especially user interaction, are still in an infant stage. The appropriateness of standardization in this case at all is also questionable.

"The scope of MHEG standard is to define the representation and encoding of multimedia and hypermedia information objects that will be interchanged as a whole within or across applications or services, by any means of interchange including storage devices, telecommunications or broadcast networks" [ISO93]. Therefore, MHEG is expected to provide a mechanism for the interchange of multimedia and hypermedia objects in a standardized manner, so that each object can be reused by a variety of different applications.

MHEG Objectives and Goals

The initial objectives of the MHEG standard are to provide abstractions for:

- real-time presentation including multimedia synchronization and interactivity.

- real-time interchange with minimal buffering using normal speed data communications.

- direct manipulation of information without any additional processing.

- linking facilities between elements of composite multimedia objects.

The above list of objectives is met by achieving a set of specific & well-defined goals that are presented hereafter. First goal is to provide a good standard framework for the development of client/server multimedia applications intended to run on a memory-constrained Client. Another important issue is to define a final-form coded representation for interchange of applications across platforms of different version and brands. This will ensure that there will be a basis for concrete conformance leveling, guaranteeing that a conformant application will run on all conformant terminals.

As for the runtime engine on the Client, the objective is to be "small" and "easy" to implement. To be free of strong constraints on the architecture of the Client.

Another requirement is to allow the development of a wide range of applications. This means also providing access to external libraries. An application using external libraries will only be partly portable.

The MHED documents should be "safe" in the sense that it cannot harm other code in the Client, nor put the Client in an abnormal state. In the standard there is provision for this purpose.

As for the authoring process the aim is to allow automatic static analysis of (final-form) application code in order to help insure bug-free applications and minimize the debugging investment needed to get a robust application. Note that this analysis should be possible to implement independently of the authoring environment. Also rapid application development is achieved by providing high-level primitives and provide a declarative paradigm for the application development.

Finally MHEG provides for:

- *simplicity*: the authoring procedure is based on a simple but useful, easy to implement framework for multimedia applications using the minimum system resources.

- *transferability*: a digital final form for presentations is defined , which may be used for exchange of the presentations between different machines no matter what make or platform.

- *extensibility*: the system should be expandable and customizable with additional application specific code, though this may make the presentation platform dependent.

Structure of MHEG

Even if MHEG is an interchange format, it is more than just a binary code. It also possesses features that suit real-time interchange in a networked environment. In MHEG we have three levels of presentation, as parts of MHEG's data interchange model: *classes*, *objects* and *run-time objects*.

MHEG classes: The encoding of MHEG is based on the architecture of the ISO presentation layer. The first part of MHEG standard contains a formal specification of all data structures in Abstract Syntax Notation (ASN.1), so-called MHEG classes. The semantics of these MHEG classes define the functionality and requirements for an MHEG runtime environment.

MHEG objects: The MHEG is object-oriented. It defines a number of classes from which instances are created when a presentation is designed. In the terminology of MHEG, these instances are MHEG objects. This way we can achieve autonomous, reusable objects. Also, it focuses on the generic structure of the objects. The basic idea is shown in Figure 1.2.

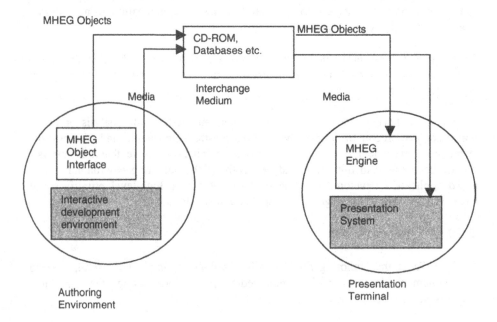

Figure 1.2. The life cycle of MHEG objects

The MHEG objects are created on a sophisticated authoring workstation, communicated to the end user through several kinds of interchange media, and executed in a presentation terminal, having scarce resources. An MHEG engine in the presentation terminal is responsible for interpreting MHEG objects to reconstruct the structure of the interactive multimedia presentation. The MHEG engine is a process or set of processes able to interpret MHEG objects. This means that the MHEG engine can decode all of the MHEG objects, handle MHEG events and links, and execute the interpreters for all MHEG's basic content object types.

As it was mentioned before, the MHEG model is object orientated, and defines a number of classes from which object instances are created when presentation is designed. There are several classes, and these are used to describe the way video is displayed, audio is reproduced and how the user can interact with the ongoing presentation. The relationship that is created between instances of these classes forms the structure of the presentation. In addition to just replaying existing multimedia data MHEG also defines some types of its own. e.g. an MHEG compliant system is able to overlay titles onto video scenes. It is also able to display menus and buttons to allow the user to make choice. The MHEG classes cover (amongst other features):

- identifiers, version no., ownership etc.,

- actions performed on target objects,

- trigger conditions and effects on target objects,

- complex actions and relationships among objects,

- synchronization, linking, and encapsulation of objects,

- the interchange of a group of objects as a single entity.

The text form of MHEG code is written in ASN 1 - abstract syntax notation version 1 - which is another ISO standard. It is quite verbose, and as such is fairly easy to read. The final form of MHEG code is binary, not textual, and this binary form must be common to all hardware platforms for the standard to work.

MHEG defines the abstract syntax through which presentations can be structured. This is the definition of data structure and the attributes in those data structures, through which two computers may communicate. In the case of a multimedia book, these two computers would be that of the author and that of the user.

Description of MHEG Classes

Since MHEG is part of ISO, the data interchange model follows the ISO philosophy, as defined in the basic reference model for Open Systems Interconnection (OSI). In particular the encoding of MHEG is based on the architecture of the OSI presentation layer. A key concept here is the separation of the abstract syntax and transfer syntax: in the abstract syntax two communicating application entities describe their data elements and data structures, defining "their universe of discourse". In this context ISO has defined a notation called Abstract Syntax Notation. The first part of the future MHEG standard contains a formal specification of al data structures in ASN.1, the so-called MHEG classes. The semantics of these MHEG classes define the functionality and requirements for an MHEG run-time environment.

The objects play a federating role, enabling different applications to share the basic information resources. These objects can be encoded using ASN.1 or SGML and will provide a common base for other CCITT recommendations, ISO and other standards, user defined architectures and applications.

MHEG defines the following object classes:

- A *content class*, for objects that contain presentable data. Content objects encapsulate media objects that are part of the presentation. For coding the content objects we use media specific standards like JPEG and MPEG.

- A *multiplexed content class*, for objects that contain sets of data that have been multiplexed into a single deliver stream.

- A *composite class*, for objects that contain more than one type of data or embedded object. Composite objects act as a "container" to group a set of MHEG objects.

- An *action class*, for objects that control actions related to data preparation, creation of run-time objects, presentation, rendition, interaction or activation of data objects. Action objects are used to exchange sets of actions to be performed between objects. Examples of actions are *prepare* to set the object in a presentable state, *run* to start the presentation and *stop* to end the presentation.

- A *link class*, for objects that define the links between data objects. Link objects are used to specify spatial, temporal and conditional relations between MHEG objects. An MHEG link is directional and connects one source object with one or more linked objects. The MHEG runtime environment (called the MHEG engine) monitors the status of the conditions and triggers the execution of actions associated with the link.

- A *script class*, for objects that contain scripts defining complex relationships between data objects. A script object is an encapsulation of scripts, which can be executed by software separate from the MHEG engine.

- A *descriptor class*, for objects that contain descriptions of interchanged objects.

- A *container class* that provides a container for grouping objects that are to be interchanged as a set.

MHEG uses the concepts of generic space and time to synchronize events. MHEG links are associative, dynamic an event driven. There are two types: object synchronization links and hyperlinks.

The exact way in which the abstract classes are displayed (e.g. check boxes and push buttons) are considered an implementation issue and are up to the designer of the MHEG engine for each platform. This is fine, since it does not affect the compatibility of different systems, just the style of display. MHEG does not define an application-programming interface for the handling of its objects. Instead mandatory and optional interface facilities are part of it. Mandatory facilities are basic actions (e.g. *run* and *stop* the presentation). Optional facilities comprise creation and access to objects (e.g. *create object, set value and get value*).

Description of MHEG Objects

The MHEG specification defines data structures, which are often reused in multiple MHEG classes. To achieve type consistency these data structures are summarized in a module called useful definitions. There are three types of identification mechanisms: external, symbolic and internal identification. The external identification is not defined by MHEG and therefore can be decoded for reference purposes without having to decode the referenced MHEG object. The symbolic identification may replace any other external or internal identification. For the internal identification the data structure MHEG identifier is used to address MHEG objects. It consists of two parts: the application identifier, a list of integer numbers, and the object number, another integer identifying objects uniquely within this application. Thus the MHEG identifier as a total uniquely identifies every single MHEG object world-wide.

The *MH-object class* is the root class of the MHEG class hierarchy. Its main purpose is to define two data structures common to all other MHEG classes. These data structures are inherited by all lower-level classes. The data structure class-identifier is used to identify the type of each class encoded by a predefined integer value. It is also possible to characterize every single MHEG object by a number of attributes.

The *content* class describes the real objects to be presented to the user. Conceptually every real content object is an atomic piece of information, containing the data necessary to present to the object to the user. Every content object is of a particular medium type. The attribute MHEG classification defines the medium type. Either the digital data can be contained in the object itself, or the object contains a unique reference to the data stream. The first case is called included data. All included data will be run through the encoder/decoder for transfer; it is subject to the usual encoding/decoding rules, similar to all other pieces of data exchanged between two MHEG entities. This is only feasible for small amounts of data, such as text for subtitles, window titles, menu lists, labels on buttons, etc. The alternative is to send the data contents as referenced data. This implies that a unique reference is encoded in the object, and the digital data will be retrieved at run-time by the MHEG-engine of the play-out site. The referencing mechanism is often also appropriate when the same large object is referenced in different multimedia presentations. This allows presentations without actually copying the data.

In addition to the encoding scheme, information on the original size of the object and the original duration of the play-out can be stored with the object. The measures for these are taken from the so-called generic space. It defines virtual coordinates on the x, y and z axes. Each axis goes from –32,768 to +32,767. At play-out time, the MHEG engine computes the physical coordinates in the object definition.

A virtual time coordinate is also defined. The interval goes from 0 to infinity and the unit is a millisecond. The temporal behavior of the play-out is created by mapping the definition of the object from the virtual time axis to the real-time requirements determined by the end-user.

The purpose of the virtual coordinates described above is to avoid device dependencies in the description of multimedia objects, such as the number of pixels in the target window, or the audio sampling rate. In addition MHEG allows one to actually transform objects during play-out. The manner in which an MHEG object can be manipulated at play-out time is determined by parameters in the encoding. Since MHEG is final form, it is not possible to modify the data itself (for example the color of the text cannot be changed).

Multimedia presentations may require access to individual streams in interleaved audio/video sequences like MPEG. Therefore a sub-class is derived from the content class called multiplexed content class. It contains or refers to the data with a description for each multiplexed stream. Single streams are accessible by a stream identifier encoded as an integer. This class also allows dynamic multiplexing of multiple streams. This is a major requirement to interface inter-stream synchronization mechanisms supported in many multimedia systems. Streams stored in individual content objects are grouped by the set-multiplex action into a single multiplexed content object.

Behavior

The *action* class is used to determine the behavior of basic MHEG objects. In object-oriented terminology an action object is actually a message sent to an MHEG object or virtual view. This message invokes the corresponding method in the object, i.e. the execution of code within the body of the object. The result of processing elementary actions is called MHEG effect. The definition of an action object is independent of the class on which it is invoked. It just represents the set of all publicly accessible MHEG objects. Implementation details are hidden from the user.

Not every action can be used on every object type. The MHEG specification contains a detailed list defining the actions allowed for each of the MHEG object types and also for virtual views. The property of polymorphism in object-oriented systems is used to allow the same action to execute on objects of different types.

Some of the actions trigger a state transition in an MHEG object, which is relevant to other objects. Reaching a certain position in the first audio triggered the appearance of the graphic, and the end of the second audio removes the graphic from the screen. In order to describe these relationships, it is important to register the state of the virtual view of the audio. For this purpose the MHEG specification contains finite state machines for important actions of this type. Most of them are quite simple because of the number of states. The preparation status represents the availability of an MHEG object. At initialization time the object is in state NOT READY. With the action PREPARE, referenced data is located, and the play-out component necessary for the presentation of the object is initialized. Then the object changes into state READY, and the content is presented on the output device using a virtual view. The action DESTROY frees all the resources allocated by the object. During processing the MHEG effect for both actions the presentation status evaluates to the intermediate state PROCESSING. Whether the object is actually output to the user depends on the presentation status of the corresponding virtual view. This status distinguishes between a RUNNING, PROCESSING and NOT-RUNNING state. Timestones allow the definition of triggers at redefined positions of a continuous stream.

A *link* class specifies under what conditions actions are sent to other objects. At execution time each link instance corresponds to an event. When the event occurs the link is activated and the action is sent to he targeted objects.

A *link* object always defines the relationship between exactly one source object and one or many target objects. The source objects and the target objects can be either MHEG objects or virtual views. The execution of a link object is triggered by he trigger condition. This condition is expressed by a state change in the source objects. As soon as the condition is fulfilled, the action objects listed within the link object body are sent to the set target objects encoded in the action object.

User Interaction

MHEG represents user interaction using two primitives: selection and modification. The former allows simple user interaction out of a predefined set of alternatives whereas the latter is used for more complex data input.

With the *selection* behavior it is possible to create events at run-time by the user. Assigning for each of the possible interaction alternatives a corresponding internal event does the definition of such events. When the user interacts with the system, the corresponding selection status changes from NOT-SELECTED to SELECTED and the assigned value is set to the attribute selection mode. A change of the selection status can be used to trigger a link object and the selection mode to evaluate the constrained condition. The selection behavior is associated with a rt-content object, for example a graphic on the screen. Hierarchical selections such as pull-down menus can also be defined.

The purpose of *modification* is the entry and manipulation of data. The modification behavior has no predetermined set of alternatives, but the result of the interaction is internally represented as a content object. The actual status of the content object is registered as the state of the object before, during and after modification.

Selection and modification are described as a behavior of a rt-content object. The style of these kinds of user interaction is defined by the interaction behavior. MHEG contains five predefined styles: button, slider, entry, field, menu and scrolling list.

Composition

It is the data structure needed to compose the multimedia presentation.

The skeleton of a presentation is given by a *composite* class. In a first step objects belonging to a certain part of the presentation have to be grouped together. The recursive definition of the composite class allows that composite objects can be part of other composite objects.

The second task of the composite class is to associate the objects in a way that they can be executed to reconstruct the encoded presentation. This is performed by four default link objects the availability-start-up/close-down and the rt-availability-start-up/close-down, which have implicit defined trigger conditions.

The MHEG standard defines three more classes: the container class, the descriptor class and the script class.

The *container* class provides a package of multiple objects in order to interchange them as a whole set, but without information how to reconstruct the presentation.

The *descriptor* class is used to encode information about the objects of a presentation. Furthermore, a descriptor object might contain quality of service information to support real-time interchange of MHEG objects. This can be used by an MHEG engine to evaluate the requirements of the presentation with respect to the available resources of the run-time platform.

The *script* class is an interface to external functions or programs. A typical application of the script class can be a database query. The query input can be encoded by suitable MHEG objects, whereas a script object is used to invoke the query executed in the script environment and to transmit data between the MHEG engine and the script environment.

MHEG Engine

Basic to MHEG is the concept of an MHEG engine. An MHEG engine consists of a set of processes that allow the presentation and application processes to interpret MHEG objects, their actions, links, status, and behavior. This mechanism provides the functions necessary to encode/decode and interpret MHEG objects handled by the presentation and user applications. These may consist of link processors, object editors, etc. The interchange of standardized MHEG objects is the feature, which enables complete integration of the MH system, despite the heterogeneous devices, systems, and applications software used at each station. Figure 1.3, shows the communication of MHEG objects between different physical implementations using their MHEG engines.

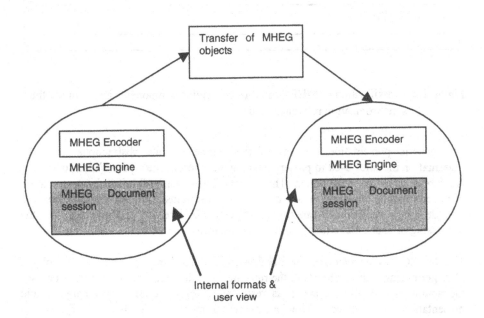

Figure 1.3. Communication of MHEG objects between MHEG engines

The MHEG engine is an implementation of the object layer. The architecture of the MHEG engine is shown in Figure 1.4 below:

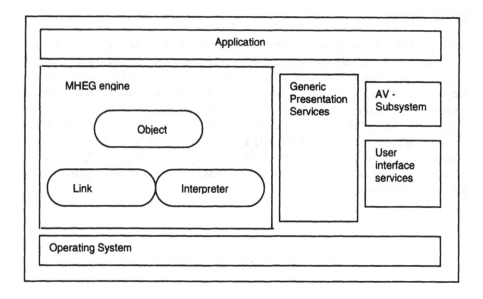

Figure 1.4. Classification of MHEG and MHEG engine components according to the synchronization reference model

The generic presentation services of the engine provide abstractions from the presentation modules used to present the content objects. The Audio Video subsystem is a stream layer implementation. This component is responsible for the presentation of the continuous media streams, e.g. audio/video streams. The user interface services provide the presentation of time-independent media, like text and graphics, and the processing of user interactions, e.g. buttons and forms.

The MHEG engine receives the MHEG objects from the application. The object manager manages these objects in the run-time environment. The interpreter processes the action objects and events. It is responsible for initiating the preparation and presentation of the objects. The link processor monitors the states of objects and triggers links, if the trigger conditions of a link are fulfilled.

The run-time system communicates with the presentation services by events. The user interface services provide events that indicate user actions. The audio/video-subsystem provides events about the status of the presentation streams, like end of the presentation of a stream or reaching a cuepoint in a stream.

A simple example of the use of MHEG would provide a single server and multiple clients capable of transferring information. In a practical example, most users would also act as providers or managers of some part of the information.

The server provides the archive for media content data: JPEG images, text, MPEG video sequences, as well as MHEG information: the links, the actions, and behavior of the objects.

An author of an MH composition supplies the user application with the structure and format of the presentation components. If, for instance, a button on the user display is 'clicked' to bring up the next object in the sequence, the object created to do this is stored on a server and is interchanged via the MHEG mechanism. Thereafter, this object and any other interchanged objects can be reused without re-transmitting the objects across the network. How this is done is left to the designer and programmer of the application processes.

 MHEG has attempted to abstract a generic set of services and functions, which would serve as the basis for the standardization of a class of MH objects, that MHEG applications must support to ensure interoperability among systems.

MHEG Standard Versions

The MHEG consists of several standards listed below. Parts 1 and 3-5 are in IS stage. MHEG-6 is currently in Committee Draft (CD).

- MHEG-1: MHEG object representation -- Base notation (ASN.1, the formal specification of all data structures in ASN.1).

- MHEG-2: HyperText Markup Language, redefined as RFC 1866, the core HTML specification defined by IETF.

- MHEG-3: MHEG script interchange representation, specifies a set of extensions for a script object interchange.

- MHEG-4: MHEG registration procedure, specifies a registration procedure for MHEG format identifier.

- MHEG-5: Support for base-level interactive application, defines the syntax and semantics of a set of object classes that can be used for interoperability of multimedia application across minimal- resources platforms.

- MHEG-6: Support for enhanced interactive application, defines some scripting extensions to MHEG-5.

Applications of MHEG

The applications to which MHEG may be used are growing, as people dream up more and more applications of multimedia. It may be used for development of development and delivery of CD-ROM based encyclopedias, interactive books for learning, video and news-on-demand systems, interactive home shopping etc.

Currently there are two mature authoring tools for MHEG-5. One is based on Asymetrix's ToolBook and the other uses Macromedia's Director.

MHEG Evaluation

One important characteristic of MHEG is that it is independent of format. This means a video content object in an MHEG document can be represented in any of the existing multimedia processing formats like MHEG or QuickTime depending on the author's preference.

An MHEG encoded document can be accessed in greater resolution upon retrieval. This has several benefits like enabling two or more persons to work on the document at the same time and allowing parts of the document to be added in at a later time. The derivatives of a MHEG document (e.g. a summary of all the sections in the document) can also be generated automatically.

The MHEG is a self-contained hypermedia –multimedia architecture that can run in environments with very small resources, such as set-top boxes where Java-enabled browsers are an overload.

1.6.2   H Y T I M E

Purpose of HyTime

When HyTime was developed, the practice of hypertext was dominated by stand-alone systems, which used different models for document structure, anchors, links, navigation, and other key features. A basic problem was the ability to interchange hypertext documents between systems with different models of hypertext. HyTime was in part conceived as a solution to the problem of content interchange between different hypertext systems. For interchange purposes, a given hypertext system could define a HyTime DTD document and then export its content as a document instance for this DTD.

HyTime specification was developed in the context of hypertext practice in the late 1980s. Additionally, musical time models, which were originally developed for the SMDL (Standard Musical Description Language) standard, were generalized in HyTime's scheduling and projection modules. Further, some facilities in HyTime are improvements to SGML (Standard Generalized Markup Language). Since this time, significant developments have occurred in the design of distributed hypermedia systems, multimedia media formats, multimedia scripting languages and authoring paradigms. Also, new distributed object frameworks are providing an environment for creating hyper-applications. These developments provide a new context in which to consider the design and use of HyTime.

HyTime defines how markup and DTDs can be used to describe the structure of hyperlinked time-based multimedia documents. HyTime does not define the format or encoding of elements. It provides the framework for defining the relationship between these elements.

HyTime provides standardized mechanisms for specifying interconnections (hyperlinks) within and between documents and other information objects, and for scheduling multimedia information in time and space. Without HyTime, such information is typically embedded in the processing instructions of hypermedia "scripts" that govern the rendition of such documents, and is therefore not usable for other forms of processing. When HyTime is used, those properties of the information are independent of specific processing, thus available for processing by applications and platforms other than the one on which the information was created.

What Is HyTime

HyTime is an ISO standard that defines an architecture for creating hypertext and hypermedia applications, while it specifies a meta-language for creating new hypermedia document types. An application designer identifies the structural elements that are suitable for the target document type. When constructing the application DTD, the designer uses the corresponding HyTime architectural forms that fit the semantics of the corresponding elements and attributes.

The meta-definition is a syntactic mechanism and does not increase the semantic capability of HyTime. The meta-DT definition of HyTime has some benefits when compared to the alternative of defining a single standard hypermedia DTD:

- *Backward compatibility with existing SGML applications,* the meta definition makes it easier to incorporate facilities of HyTime into existing SGML DTDs without modifying the names of existing elements and attributes.

- *Multiple HyTime-based DTDs,* different application DTDs can be defined as applications of HyTime. Similarly, the instances of many different DTDs can be included in the same HyTime hypermedia document set.

- *The name space for element generic identifiers (GI) is more flexible,* the HyTime meta-DTD doesn't define any GIs, and more than one application GI can use a HyTime ETF (Element Type Form). Additionally, an application can define its own non-HyTime GIs, and has complete control over attribute names.

The meta definition, however, complicates the use of HyTime since it leads to an additional level of indirection. That is, the designer of a tag set must conceptually work at one additional level, the meta-DTD level, when defining elements and attributes for the application DTD.

Since many hypermedia applications share structural and composition requirements - in particular time, space, and hyperlinks - a standard description of these components of applications means that less custom code is needed to deliver the application. At the same time, HyTime is rather inadequate as regards to presentation and interaction, and so is an incomplete way of describing most existing hypermedia and multimedia documents. Consequently it is impossible to deliver any hypermedia application by providing only a HyTime document instance and DTD to a HyTime engine. Unlike SGML applications, which operate with a document instance, DTD, and style sheet, typical HyTime applications appear to require custom software beyond the HyTime engine. This custom software is not just for the media specific presentation. Custom software is required for all time, space, and interaction semantics for presentation. This means that each time a new HyTime DTD is created for a new application, some custom presentation software must also be developed. By adopting certain conventions, a significant portion of the presentation software could be automatically generated, but it is not a complete solution.

HyTime defines the following aspects of hypermedia document structure: i. addressing of document objects, ii. relationships between document objects, iii. numeric measurements of document objects.

SGML and HyTime

HyTime is to a great extend based on SGML (*Standardized General Markup Language*), which means that it is designed using SGML as the notation language and defines a number of functions related directly to SGML constructs.

SGML is designed for document interchange, whereby the document structure is of great importance, but the layout is a local matter. The logical structure is defined by markup commands that are inserted in the text. The markups divide the text into SGML elements. For each SGML document a data type definition (DTD) exists, which declares the element types of the document, the attributes of the elements and how the instances are hierarchically related. A typical use of SGML is in the publishing industry, where an author is responsible for the content and structure of the document and the publisher is responsible for the layout. Since the content of the document is not restricted by SGML, elements can be of type text, picture or any other multimedia data.

HyTime was developed by the same committee that created the SGML standard, and the primary target of HyTime is the SGML community. In particular, HyTime itself is defined as an SGML meta-DTD (Data Type Definition) and use of HyTime requires use of SGML.

HyTime inherits from SGML the ability to define, multiple document models, open and integrated documents, and document structure independently of document presentation.

In terms of functionality, however, HyTime extends the power of SGML in many ways:

- *addressing*: With HyTime, everything becomes addressable in any convenient terms, including both SGML and non-SGML information components, at any granularity.

- *validating*: With HyTime, attribute values and data content can be checked for conformance to arbitrary lexical models, references can be constrained to refer to particular kinds of things, etc.

- *multiple inheritance* (SGML architectures): HyTime greatly enhances the object-oriented features of SGML. Elements can inherit semantic and syntactic features not only from the governing DTD, but also from any number of other DTDs, called ``base architectures''. This makes it possible, for example, for software written to support semantic processing of information conforming to a particular DTD to be re-used in many other contexts.

- *linking, scheduling, and component re-use*: HyTime allows semantics to be conferred upon any SGML or non-SGML information component. For example, a phrase in a read-only document can become an anchor or hyperlink such that a traversal can be initiated from it, even though no markup is added to the phrase itself. Other semantics include re-use in other documents (without copying), scheduling of the component's rendition in time and/or space (hence the name ``HyTime''), and association of access policies. HyTime is the standard way to re-use all kinds of information, and it will form the basis of the most powerful and general information management systems for the foreseeable future.

Scope of HyTime

This International Standard defines a language and underlying model for the representation of "hyperdocuments" that line and synchronize static and dynamic (time-based) information contained in multiple conventional and multimedia document and information objects. The language is known as the "Hypermedia/Time-based Structuring Language", or "HyTime"

HyTime can represent time in both the abstract or "musical" sense, and in user-defined real-time units. It also provides a way of relating the two, so that elements of time-dependent documents can be synchronized.

This facility extends to the representation of multimedia information the power, once limited to conventional documents, to distinguish intrinsic information content from style considerations

HyTime's techniques for representing the time model are equally applicable to spatial and other domains; all are treated as systems for measuring along different axes of a coordinate space. Arbitrary cross-references and access paths based on external interactions ("hypermedia links") are also supported

HyTime's time representation contains sufficient information to derive the duration of both control ("gestural") data (e.g. control information for audio or video hardware) and visual data (e.g., a music score, presentation storyboard, or television script)

The media formats and data notations of objects in a HyTime hyperdocument can include formatted and unformatted documents, audio and video segments, still images, and object-oriented graphics, among others. Users can specify the positions and sizes of occurrences of objects in space and time, using a variety of measurement units and granularities. Temporal requirements of applications, ranging from animation to project management, can be supported by choosing appropriate measurement granules.

This International Standard does not address the representation of audio or video content data, but simply defines the means by which the start-time and duration of such data can be synchronized with other digitized information. Nor does it specify the layout process by which occurrences of unformatted documents and other information objects can be made to fit the positions and sizes specified for them.

HyTime is designed for flexibility and extensibility. Optional subsets can be implemented, alone or in conjunction with user-defined extensions.

The Hypermedia/Time-based Structuring Language (HyTime) is an SGML application conforming to International Standard ISO 8879 - Standard Generalized Markup Language. The hyperdocument interchange format recommended in this International Standard is ISO 9069, the SGML Document Interchange Format (SDIF).

Field of Application

The field of application of HyTime is "integrated open hypermedia", the "bibliographic model" of hyperlinks where an author can, by a suitable reference, link to any other entity of the documents [ISO92].

HyTime aims to be the infrastructure of platform-independent information interchanges for hypermedia synchronized and non-synchronized multimedia applications. Application developers will use HyTime constructs to design their information structures and objects, and the HyTime language to represent them for interchange.

The HyTime language is not intended for encoding the internal representation of information on which application programs act while executing.

The Modules of HyTime

A stated objective of HyTime's support declaration is to permit an application to require only the relevant subsets of HyTime. HyTime is designed to be used modularly. Only those portions of HyTime, which are appropriate to a given document or application, need to be supported. A HyTime document may be a multimedia document, a hypertext document, a time-based or space-based only document, or it may be any combination of these. The primary modules support:

- basic utility functions (the *base module*),

- the indication of segments of information, wherever they may be, (the *location address module*),

- the declarations of hypermedia links, anchors (the *hyperlink module*) and

- the specification of time and space relationships (the *finite coordinate space - FCS - module*).

Two additional modules can de added to the *finite coordinate space module*: the *event projection* module and the *object modification* module.

The latter are used to specify the rendition of HyTime documents. The base module must always be supported by any HyTime compliant system. In addition, under most circumstances, at least one of the other modules must also be supported in order to take advantage of HyTime's standard semantics. In the following there is a brief presentation of the most relevant to the theme of the book modules.

Base Module

The base module includes features that support the facilities of other modules or facilities that are (sometimes optionally) available regardless of which of the other modules are supported. The base module includes:

- Hyperdocument management facilities, required for all other HyTime facilities: SGML itself, with all inherent representational and document management abilities

- HyTime identification facilities, which permit the replacement of HyTime specific identifiers with user-defined identifiers

- Means for specifying application-defined expressions, called xenoforms, in such a way to identify the notation used.

- Coordinate addressing facility, which allows the specification of dimension(s) and position of events and document locations, to be addressed by position

- Optional means for specifying activity-tracking policies. HyTime's location address and hyperlink modules are designed to allow literally anything to become an end of a hyperlink.

- Other optional basic utilities intended to provide syntactically economical means of declaring default attribute values and definition tables.

Location Address Module

SGML provides a simple way to refer to particular elements in the same document, using its unique identifier facility. An identifier (#ID) attribute data type can be used to provide any instance of an element with a name unique to that instance. The fact that the identifier is unique is guaranteed only within the current document. Therefore, each document is known to have its own "name space". Addressing is accomplished in this case by using an "identifier reference" (#IDREF) attribute data type, the value of which is the same as the value of the #ID-type attribute that appears on some other element within the same document (i.e. the same name space).

Using the SGML #ID-#IDREF combination it is possible to represent the address of hypertext link endpoints in a standard fashion without the extensions provided by the HyTime location address module. However the usefulness of the #ID-#IDREF addressing method is limited: only the contents of entire elements within the same local document can be addressed and only when those elements are provided with unique identifiers. HyTime extends SGML's reference capability to accommodate those cases in which no unique identifier for an information object exists in the local document's name space. HyTime provides location address architectural forms (i.e., pointer), which have unique local identifiers, and which contain the information needed to accomplish the task of locating the data.

When a hyperdocument author wants to refer to an object which does not have a unique identifier in the local name space, the author can create a location address element, which links the object in question with a unique local identifier. A HyTime-conforming application will recognize the identifier as an address element, and it will know how to use the information it contains to "resolve" the address, i.e., to recover the information pointed at by the address element. Address elements can be chained and aggregated according to the nature and complexity of the addressing job.

The ability to resolve HyTime addresses in a given notation is dependent on software that can interpret that notation in terms of the abstractions that HyTime uses for all addressing. HyTime supports three types of addressing: by position in a coordinate space, by name, and by semantic construct.

Hyperlink Module

There are five kinds of hyperlink defined in HyTime, which are designed to meet generic as well as some specialized hyperlink needs: independent link (ilink), property link (plink), contextual link (clink), aggregate location link (agglink), and spanlink.

Finite Coordinate Space (FCS) Module

The Finite coordinate space module provides for the scheduling of objects. Optional projection and modification modules, for which the FCS module is prerequisite, provide mechanisms for controlling or guiding the rendition of scheduled documents (or parts of documents). The RCS has two modules:

- *Event projection module:* The Event projection module facilities are used to specify how the positions and extends of events in one FCS are mapped onto another.

- *Object Modification Module:* the Object Modification Module provides a way to specify the orderly application of object modifiers and combinations of object modifiers

HyTime Addressing

HyTime works with objects in finite coordinate spaces and objects within trees. A HyTime document usually does not directly include the media data but refers to them via references. HyTime primarily addresses the problem of hyperlinking as a problem of addressing, in other words, locating objects in space or time. A key aspect of addressing is the use of queries to find things based on their properties. HyTime supports addresses to identify a certain piece of information within an element, linking facilities to establish links between parts of elements and temporal and spatial alignment specifications to describe relationships between media objects. The linking allows creating links between parts of information that are for example fundamental in hypermedia applications. Alignment supports placement of portions of information within finite coordinate systems.

Application structure, which cannot be represented with HyTime facilities, can be represented by defining application specific elements and attributes.

Coordinate Addressing

Coordinate spaces are always defined in terms of quanta, in other words, non-divisible integer units. A one-dimensional coordinate space can be represented as a number line. A two-dimensional coordinate space can be represented as a matrix.

Dimension specifications are used to locate within a single dimension or along a single axis. In a multi-dimensional space, an extent must be created, which contains a "dimensions list" for each axis and defines the extent of the region of the finite coordinate space.

The area within a given coordinate space that a dimension specification is actually addressing is called the ADDRESSABLE RANGE. The addressable range always has well-defined boundaries, in other words, a start and an end. Knowing where the end of the addressable range one can specify locations relative to the end of the range as well as relative to the start of the range.

The start and extent values have special meanings when a minus sign is used with them.

When the start quantum is negative, it indicates that counting start at the end of the addressable range rather than at the beginning. When the extent value is negative, it indicates that the extent is from the end of the range, not the starting quanta.

Node-List and Tree Addressing

HyTime also provides tree-like organization structures and location mechanisms for locating objects within trees. In HyTime terms, a tree represents a hierarchical collection of NODES, where a node is to a tree what a quantum is to a coordinate-space: simply a way of defining where something is located in a tree.

Nodes can also be organized into lists, called NODE LISTS. Nodes have the special property that they can be the roots of trees.

The typical use of tree locations in HyTime applications is to locate elements within SGML documents, as SGML documents are always hierarchical structures of elements and are therefore naturally represented as trees. Other types of data can be addressed as trees or node-lists by providing notation handlers for those data notations that can translate node and tree addresses into real addresses for that data type. For example, a notation handler for PostScript data could allow addressing of pages in a PostScript listing as nodes in a node list. It is up to the implementers of   a given HyTime system to provide this sort of functionality.

Nodes can thus be organized or viewed as members of node lists of trees. Nodes can be located by any of the following location mechanisms: Tree location address, list location address, path location address and relative location address.

Semantic Locations

Semantic locations provide means of locating aspects of objects that are unique to their semantic roles, as opposed to their structural roles. Semantic location methods are:

- Property locations (*proploc*), locate values of object properties, such as attribute values and generic identifiers.

- Non-SGML data notations can have properties defined for them using the HyTime property definition constructs.

- Notation-specific locations (*notloc*), locate into data in a given notation using addressing methods specific to that notation, as opposed to using normal HyTime addressing that is interpreted by a notation processor that understands HyTime addressing.

- Bibliographic locations (*bibloc*), locate elements that are not directly addressable by the system, normally references to real objects, such as printed books, people, and the like.

Proploc is the semantic location method used most often. Notloc is a sort of "escape" that allows addressing into data notations for which generalized HyTime support has not been provided.

Property Location Addressing

SGML elements have properties as defined by ISO 8879, e.g., the generic identifier and any declared attributes. In addition, application designers may define other properties for elements or for other data types. Property definition is done in HyTime using the HyTime property definition element form. New properties can be defined and it can be attached names by which they can be referred to from a proploc.

Notation Location Addressing

Notation locations are location address specifications unique to a particular data notation, rather than being standard HyTime dimension references or queries. Notation locations must be used to address into data notations for which a HyTime-knowledgeable notation processor is not available.

The main problem with notation locations is that they are directly tied to a specific notation and are thus not very interchangeable.

In a pure HyTime system, for each supported notation there would be a least one notation processor that would accept standard HyTime address (dimension specifications or data locations, for example) and would know how to transform the

HyTime specification into real locations is the specific data notation. For example, we consider that somebody wants to address words in text regardless of the format that text is stored in, because it could be in any one of several proprietary formats. If each format has a HyTime notation processor available, a simple data location address with a defined quanta of WORD can be used without worrying about how to actually find words in the actual data, because the notation processor would handle that transparently.

However, if there was a format for which there was no HyTime-knowledgeable notation processor, to address words, the address in the specific notation has to be specified.

Addressing Media Objects

The nature of multimedia documents is that much of the content of the document will be in binary files external to the HyTime document. HyTime's role in a multimedia document is to connect all the pieces of the presentation and represent the structural relationships between them. Important relationships may include spatial, temporal, composition, transformation, and hyperlinking. All media and non-HyTime files will be interpreted and presented by processes separate from the HyTime processing system. HyTime is neutral with respect to the formats used by non-HyTime files. It does provide architectural forms for supporting location addressing of objects in non-HyTime formats, and for representing hierarchical external entity structure when the media entity of interest is embedded in a container entity.

HyTime Engine

The task of a HyTime engine is to take the output of an SGML parser, to recognize architectural forms and to perform the HyTime-specific and application independent processing. Typical subtasks of the HyTime engine are hyperlink resolution, object addressing, parsing of measures and schedules, and transformation of schedules and dimensions. The resulting information is then provided to the HyTime application.

The HyTime engine, HyOctane [Koe93], developed at the University of Massachusetts at Lowel, has the following architecture: an SGML parser takes as input the application data type definition that is used for the document and the HyTime document instance. It stores the document object's markups and contents, as well as the application's DTD in the SGML layer of the database. The HyTime engine takes as input the information stored in the SGML layer of the database. It identifies the architectural forms, resolves addresses from the location address module, handles the functions of the scheduling module and performs the mapping specified in the rendition module. The latter is used to specify how the events of a source FCS, that typically provides a generic presentation description, are transformed to a target FCS that is used for a particular presentation. The HyTime engine stores the information about elements of the document that are instances of architectural forms in the

HyTime layer of the database. The application layer of the database stores the objects and their attributes, as defined by the DTD. An application presenter gets the information it needs for the presentation of the database content, including the links between objects and the presentation coordinates to use for the presentation, from the database.

Prior to its standardization, little of HyTime was validated by implementation. Subsequent to its standardization, only a few implementations of subsets of HyTime exist, in part because of the complexity of the specification. Complete validation would require significant experience with:

- Interchange between different hypermedia systems.

- Multimedia DTD design.

- Creation of large heterogeneous hypermedia document collections.

HyTime Evaluation

In the following we summarize HyTime's features. Hypermedia applications share structural and composition requirements - in particular time, space, and hyperlinks. Therefore a standard description of these components of applications means that less custom code is needed to deliver the application. On the other hand, HyTime does not cover properly presentation and interaction issues, and so is an incomplete way of describing most existing hypermedia and multimedia documents. Consequently it is impossible to deliver any hypermedia application by providing only a HyTime document instance and DTD to a HyTime engine. Unlike SGML applications which operate with a document instance, DTD, and style sheet, typical HyTime applications require custom software beyond the HyTime engine. This custom software is not just for the media specific presentation. Custom software is required for all time, space, and interaction semantics for presentation. This means that each time a new HyTime DTD is created for a new application, some custom presentation software must also be developed.

HyTime focuses on representing structure of both the document hypergraph and the nodes of the hypergraph. Delivery issues including interaction and presentation facilities, integration with computation engines and other applications, and authoring paradigms are outside the scope of HyTime.

Time is a fundamental compositional notion in multimedia and hypermedia documents. Although HyTime has a scheduling module, there are no explicit time or space axes, but simply arbitrary dimensions which the application is free to interpret as it wishes. For example, one might place a series of images in a HyTime axis named "t" and associate units of seconds with this axis, but HyTime doesn't prescribe whether these images should be shown in time order to the user, or whether they just happen to have an intrinsic chronological relation, such as the order in which they were painted by an artist. The interpretation of the axis in time or space is left to the application.

One important area is the ability to represent synchronization relationships. In multimedia documents, the specification of a synchronization relationship between two or more media objects allows the presentation system to properly coordinate synchronization recovery in the event of unexpected delay in one or more of the media channels.

In the case of temporal structure, HyTime provides facilities, which can be used to represent both temporal composition and temporal synchronization, but the temporal semantics are left to the application to determine.

1.6.3   Comparison of MHEG and Hytime

MHEG and HyTime are ISO standards. They both serve the same purpose, that is, to enable hypermedia and multimedia systems interchange data in a manageable format. They tell system developers how to encode and structure hypermedia and time-based data.

Between MHEG and HyTime there are similarities as well as differences:

- Both, MHEG and HyTime deal with synchronization issues in multimedia applications.

- In comparison to MHEG, HyTime does not represent interaction and presentation aspects of multimedia content. HyTime focuses on representing structure of the hypergraph and the nodes of the hypergraph.

- The implementation experience with both MHEG and HyTime indicates that an MHEG engine is significantly simpler and requires less memory, an important consideration for consumer devices. Typical HyTime applications require custom software beyond the HyTime engine.

- MHEG uses an object-oriented approach to achieve active, autonomous, reusable objects. Although HyTime considers architectural forms as object – classes, which are identified by the value of the HyTime attribute it is not an object-oriented model.

- With HyTime there is no explicit time or space axes, but simply arbitrary dimensions which the application is free to interpret as it wishes. Also, HyTime has the ability to represent synchronization relationships.

For multimedia applications there are significant limitations with regard to interactive behavior, support for scripting language integration and presentation aspects and many developments have to be made in this direction.

1.6.4   SMIL

The key to HTML success was that attractive hypertext content could be created without requiring a sophisticated authoring tool. Synchronized Multimedia Integration Language (SMIL)[Smil98] aims at the same objective for synchronized hypermedia. It is an upcoming standard for synchronized multimedia to be presented in a WWW browser. SMIL allows integration of a set of independent multimedia objects into a synchronized multimedia presentation. A typical SMIL presentation has the following features:

- the presentation is composed of several components that are accessible via a URL, e.g. files stored on a Web server.

- the components are of different media types, such as audio, video, image or text.

- interaction support in terms of simple events. This implies that the begin and end times of different components have to be synchronized with events produced by internal objects or by external user interaction. Also simple user interaction is supported. The user can control the presentation by using control buttons known from video-recorders, such as stop, fast-forward and rewind. Additional functions are "random access", i.e. the presentation can be started anywhere, and "slow motion", i.e. the presentation is played slower than at its original speed.

- support for hyperlinks, the user can follow hyper-links embedded in the presentation

Hereafter we will refer to the SMIL elements related to the themes of this book, such as object specification, interaction handling and spatiotemporal synchronization of media objects in the framework of an interactive scenario.

Media Object Elements

A SMIL document may contain audio, image, video and text objects (*elements*). The media object elements allow the inclusion of external components into a SMIL presentation.

The names "audio", "video", "text" and "img" are synonyms for *ref*. They serve to improve the readability of the document. The player does not derive the type of the media object from the name of the media object element. This is important when the URL points to the description of a media object file rather than to the object itself.

Anchors and links can be attached to visual media objects (such as media objects typically included via the "video", "text" and "img" elements). This is achieved by putting the appropriate *anchor* elements between the start tag and the end tag of the media object.

The media object is defined by its attributes *src* (the URL of the media object), and *type* (optional, MIME type of the media object referenced by the src attribute).

It is also possible to define its duration through the *dur* element that specifies the difference between the begin time and the end time of the media object element. For continuous media objects (e.g. audio or video objects), the default value is the intrinsic duration of the media object.

In the case that the author wants part of the object to be presented, it is possible through the *range* attribute, which specifies that only a sub-clip of a continuous media object (such as audio, video or another presentation) should be played. A range has the general form <begin-timestamp> "-" <end-timestamp>. If the begin-timestamp is missing, the clip starts at the beginning of the temporal media object. If the end-timestamp is missing, the clip ends with the end of the temporal media object.

Synchronization Attributes

The synchronization attributes "begin" and "end" can be added to any schedule element in order to change the default begin and end times of the element. A synchronization attribute can be an *offset value* or a qualified *event*.

In the case of an offset value, its semantics depends on the parent of the element containing the synchronization attribute. If the parent is a parallel element, the value defines a time-offset from the beginning of the parallel element while in the case of a sequential element, the value defines a time-offset from the end of the predecessor element.

If the value of a synchronization attribute is an event generated by an element, the attribute specifies that an element should begin or end when a particular event occurs in another element. This element must be a sibling of the element with the synchronization attribute. The following events are defined for all schedule elements: *begin*, *end* and *clock-val*.

The *begin* event is generated when the element becomes active. The *end* event is triggered when the element becomes inactive. The *clock-val* element is triggered when the clock associated with an element reaches a particular value. This clock starts at 0 when the element begins to be displayed. It is defined as follows. If the element is a media object, its associated clock gives the media time of the object. The media time of an object may differ from the presentation time that elapsed since the object's display started e.g. due to rendering or network delays. If the element is a seq element, its associated clock gives the presentation time elapsed since the sequence element started. If the element is a par element that ends when an especially designated element ends (endsync=id-ref), the associated clock is equal to the clock associated with this element. Otherwise, the clock is equal to the presentation time that has elapsed since the parallel element started.

Temporal Synchronization

SMIL provides temporal synchronization capabilities trough the *schedule* elements which can be *composite* (parallel, sequential) or *atomic* (media-object). Schedule elements have a *begin* and an *end* time. For an element A they can be determined either by the composite element which contains A, or by synchronization attributes contained within the start tag of A. The player keeps track of a presentation clock that advances at the speed of the presentation and measures presentation time.

The par Element

This element is used in order to represent parallel presentation of two or more media objects (referred to as *children*). The syntax of the element as it is described in [SMI98] follows:

```
parallel           = "<par" "par-attribute (">" "par-content "</par" ">" | "/>")
par-content        = schedule | switch | link | xml-Misc
par-attribute      = id | endsync | sync | dur | repeat | fill | channel |
                     "sync-attribute | "switch-param-attribute
endsync            = "endsync" "=" (<">endsync-value<"> | <'>endsync-value<'>)
endsync-value          = "first" | "last" |  id-ref
id-ref             = "id(" id-value ")"
sync               = "sync" "=" sync-value
dur                = "dur" "=" (<">clock-val<"> | <'>clock-val<'>)
clock-val          = full-clock-val | partial-clock-val | timecount-val
full-clock-val     = hours ":" minutes ":" seconds ["." units]
partial-clock-val  = minutes ":" seconds ["." units]
```

By default, the end time of a parallel element is equal to the maximum end time of all children in the parallel element. If none of the children has a known end time, then the end time and the duration of the parallel element are also unknown. In this case, the parallel element is terminated by an external event, for example when the user hits a "stop" button. The default end time of a parallel element can be overridden by using the endsync, the dur or the end attribute.

If the begin/end time of a child in a parallel element is unknown, it is set to the begin/end time of the parallel element. In a par-element it is possible to define how accurately the children in a parallel group are synchronized in case of playback delays. This is achieved through the optional *sync* attribute which additionally determines what to do if the parallel group contains two or more continuous media types such as audio or video, and one of them experiences a delay. The attribute can have the following values: *hard* (the player must synchronize the children in the parallel group to a common clock) and *soft* (each child of the parallel element has its own clock, which runs independently of the clocks of other children in the parallel element). The default value for sync is specified within a "meta" element. If no default value is specified, the default value is implementation-dependent. In the case of hard synch, if there is a delay in video either the audio is stopped or some video frames are dropped. The exact behavior is again implementation-dependent. Alternatively, in the case of soft sync, the optional *endsync* attribute specifies that the parallel element depends on the end time of one of its children. The attribute can have the following values:

- *last,* which is the default, and imposes that the parallel element ends when all of its children have ended

- *first,* the parallel element ends as soon one of its children ends. In this case the exact duration of the parallel element can only be determined at run-time

- *id-ref,* the parallel group ends at the same time as the child identified by the id ends

The optional attribute *dur* specifies the difference between the begin time and the end time of the parallel element. This attribute is ignored if the par element also contains an endsync attribute. The optional attribute *fill* has an effect when an element is contained within another *par* or *seq* (sequential) element. It determines what happens with "slack-time" that may occur once the duration of an element has ended. The exact semantics depend on the parent element: If the parent element is a par, the fill attribute specifies the behavior of an element when its duration is shorter than the duration of the par element. If the parent element is a seq element, the fill attribute specifies the behavior of an element when the begin of its successor is delayed. The attribute can have the following values:

- *remove,* default, the element is removed from the display when its duration ends

- *freeze,* in this case if the element is a non-continuous visual media object (e.g. a text or an image), the element continues to be displayed after its duration has ended. If the element is a continuous visual media object (e.g. a video), the last state of the media object (e.g. the last frame) is continued to be displayed. If the element is an audio object, this value has no effect. If the element is a par element, its children are "frozen". If the element is a seq element, the last element in the sequence is "frozen".

- *loop,* the element is repeated from the beginning.

Through the "repeat" attribute, SMIL supports consecutive presentations of a media object that specifies the number of times an element should be repeated. A value of "0" indicates that the element is repeated an infinite number of times. The default value is 1.

The seq Element

This element is used in order to represent *sequential* presentation of two or more children. The syntax of the element as it is described in [SMI98] follows:

```
sequential   = "<seq" "seq-attribute (">" "seq-content "</seq" ">" I "/>")
seq-content         = schedule I switch I link I xml-Misc
seq-attribute = id I dur I repeat I fill I sync-attribute I
                    switch-param-attribute
```

The begin and end time of a child object in a seq element construct, supports sequential synchronization. It contains the following default values: the *begin* time of the *first* child is set to the begin time of the seq element, the *begin* times of all other children are set to the end times of their lexical predecessors. The default value for the end time of a seq element is the end time of the last element contained in the sequence.

Error Handling

SMIL provides some error handling features basically attached to syntactic features. If an element contains "begin", "end" and "dur" attributes, the "dur" attribute is ignored. A continuous media object has an intrinsic duration. If it also has either a dur attribute, or a begin and an end attribute, the element's duration is the minimum of its intrinsic duration, and the duration defined by the attributes.

If a parallel element contains both an "endsync" attribute and an "end" attribute, the element ends at the minimum of the end times specified by these two attributes.

All documents containing errors caused by synchronization attributes are invalid. Possible errors are, for example, loops in the graph specifying begin or end times, begin times that lie after end times, events generated by non-sibling elements, sequential elements in which elements overlap, a reference to a clock value that exceeds the duration of an element, conflicts between begin/end times and the duration of an object, etc.

A salient feature of SMIL is the switch element, which allows an author to specify a set of alternative elements from which only one element should be chosen.

The switch element can be used, for example, to express that the audio track of a video is available in different languages. More generally, the elements within a switch differ with respect to one or more parameter values (e.g. language, bitrate).

Hyperlinking

SMIL provides for specification and manipulation of links with the link element. The link element allows the description of navigational links between objects. SMIL linking is based on the linking concepts described in the XML Linking draft (XLL). This specification uses the terms *resource, linking element, locator* and *in-line link* as defined in XLL. SMIL provides only for *in-line* link elements. Links are limited to uni-directional single-headed links (i.e. all links have exactly one source and one destination resource). All links in SMIL are activated by the user.

A SMIL document may involve other (non-SMIL) applications or plug-ins. For example, a SMIL browser may use an HTML plug-in to display an embedded HTML page. Vice versa, an HTML browser may use a SMIL plug-in to display a SMIL document embedded in an HTML page.

In such presentations, links may be defined by documents at different levels and conflicts may arise. In this case, the link defined by the containing document should take precedence over the link defined by the embedded object. Note that since this might require communication between the browser and the plug-in, SMIL implementations may choose not to comply with this recommendation.

If a link is defined in an embedded SMIL document, traversal of the link affects only the embedded SMIL document. If a link is defined in a non-SMIL document that is embedded in a SMIL document, link traversal can only affect the presentation of the embedded document and not the presentation of the containing SMIL document. This restriction may be released in future versions of SMIL.

Anchors

HTML image maps have demonstrated that it is useful to associate links with spatial subparts of an object. SMIL provides for various types of anchors so that linking becomes flexible. This need is fulfilled by the *anchor* element. The anchor element realizes similar functionality for SMIL:

- The anchor element allows associating a link destination to spatial and temporal subparts of a media object, using the *href* attribute (in contrast, the *a* element only allows associating a link with the whole media object).

- The anchor element allows that a subpart of the media object can become the destination of a link, using the *id* attribute.

- The anchor element allows breaking up an object into spatial subparts, using the *coords* attribute.

- The anchor element allows breaking up an object into temporal subparts, using the *begin* and *end* attributes. The values of the begin and end attributes are relative to the beginning of the media object.

- Some media formats such as CGM or HTML already provide an internal mechanism for associating an identifier with a subparts of a media object expressed in this format. The anchor element allows accessing these subparts, using the *iid* attribute.

The spatial attributes of the link is specified by the attribute that defines a rectangle within the display area of a visual media object. Coordinates are relative to the top left corner of the visual media object. If a coordinate is specified as a percentage value, it is relative to the total width or height of the media object display area. When two rectangles overlap, the one with the higher *z-index* value takes precedence. This attribute specifies the stacking order of elements in the case that their rendering spaces overlap. Its value is a non-negative integer. Elements are stacked in order of increasing z-index value (i.e. highest z-index value on top). The default value is 0.

When two elements have the same z-index and overlap both in time and in space, their stacking order is defined by the following rules:

- If the display of an element A starts later than the display of an element B, A is stacked on top of B (temporal order).
- If the display of the elements starts at the same time, and an element A occurs later in the SMIL document text than an element B, A is stacked on top of B (textual order).

Some illustrative examples follow:

Associating links with temporal subparts

In the following example, the duration of a video clip is split into two subintervals. A different link is associated with each of these subintervals.

```
<video src="http://www.w3.org/SMIL">
  <anchor href="http://www.w3.org/AudioVideo" begin="0s" end="5s"/>
  <anchor href="http://www.w3.org/Style"     begin="5s" end="10s"/>
</video>
```

Associating links with spatial subparts

In the following example, the screen-space taken up by a video clip is split into two regions. A different link is associated with each of these regions.

```
<video src="http://www.w3.org/SMIL">
  <anchor href="http://www.w3.org/AudioVideo" coords="0%,0%,50%,50%"/>
  <anchor href="http://www.w3.org/Style"      coords="50%,50%,100%,100%"/>
</video>
```

Jumping to a subpart of an object

The following example contains a link from an element in a presentation A to the middle of another presentation B. This would play presentation B starting from the point where the designated fragment begins (i.e. the presentation would start as if the user had fast-forwarded to the beginning of the designated fragment in the "Olympic games" video).

presentation A:

```
<a href="http://www.anode.somecountry/mm/presentationB#tim">
  <video id="graph" src="rtsp://ofo.com/graph.gif" channel="l_window"/>
</a>
```

presentation B:

```
<video src="http://www.w3.org/CoolStuff">
  <anchor id="joe" begin="0s" end="5s"/>
  <anchor id="tim" begin="5s" end="10s"/>
</video>
```

2. Modeling Interactive Multimedia Documents

It recognized that data base support is essential and it requires the enrichment of the DBMS models with new complex data types that are created by combining basic multimedia data types. Special emphasis must be put in the interactive nature of a multimedia document and in the spatiotemporal orchestration requirements. As for the interaction, it includes users and DBMS interaction with multimedia data. The data is no longer static but made dynamic by support for user (and multi-user) applications , and system interaction. In addition data can interact and affect other data.

The main issues which multimedia database management researchers/designers need to face include:

- Development of sophisticated conceptual models, which are rich in their semantic capabilities to represent complex multimedia objects and express their synchronization requirements. A transformation from models to database scheme is then needed. Subsequently one also needs to specify the object retrieval algorithms.

- Designing multimedia query languages which are not only powerful enough to handle various manipulation functions for multimedia objects but also simple in handling user's interaction for these functions

- Designing powerful indexing and organization techniques for multimedia data.

- Developing efficient storage layout models to manage real-time multimedia data.

A multimedia information repository includes the following information layers: the raw multimedia data, the multimedia objects model (structure and behavior of multimedia objects) and the multimedia application model (incorporating scenaria based on events and composition). A number of attempts have been made to develop conceptual models for representing multimedia objects. These models can be classified into five categories, namely (Chafoor, 1994): graphical models, Petri-Net based models, object oriented models, language-based models, and temporal abstraction models.

An Interactive Multimedia Document (IMD) involves a variety of individual multimedia objects presented according to a set of specifications called the IMD scenario. The multimedia objects that participate in the IMD are transformed, either spatially or temporally, in order to be presented according to author's requirements. Moreover, the author has to define the spatial and temporal order of objects within the document context and the relationships among them. Finally, the way that the user will interact with the presentation session as well as the way that the application will treat application or system events, has to be defined. The related application domains are quite challenging and demanding. Among others, these can be: interactive TV, digital movies, and virtual reality applications.

In the framework of IMDs we consider the following as cornerstone concepts in a modeling effort:

- Events: they are the fundamental means of *interaction* in the context of the IMD and are raised by user actions, by objects participating in the IMD or by the system. They may be simple (i.e. not decomposable in the IMD context) or complex, and have attached their spatiotemporal signature (i.e. the space and the time they occurred). For more details refer to [VB97].

- Spatiotemporal Composition: it is an essential part of an IMD and represents the spatial and temporal ordering of media objects in the corresponding domain. At this point, the issue of spatial and temporal relationships among the objects is critical [VTS98].

- Scenario: it stands for the integrated behavioral contents of the IMD, i.e. what kind of events the IMD will consume and what presentation actions will be triggered as a result. In our approach a scenario consists of a set of self-standing functional units (scenario tuples) that include: triggering events (for start and stop), presentation actions (in terms of spatio temporal compositions) to be carried out in the context of the scenario tuple, and related synchronization events (i.e. events that get triggered when a scenario tuple starts or stops).

2.1   Interaction

Interaction is one of the cornerstone entities of a multimedia document. It represents the information flowing between the various players in an IMD session. We will use the event concept to represent interaction in this context.

The concept of events is defined in several research areas. In the area of Active Databases [G94, GJS92, CM93] an event is defined as an instantaneous *happening of interest* [GJS92]. An event is caused by some action that happens at a specific point in time and may be atomic or composite. In the multimedia literature, events are not uniformly defined. In [SW95] events are defined as a temporal composition of objects, thus they have a temporal duration. In other proposals for multimedia composition and presentation, e.g., [HFK95, VS96], events correspond to temporal instances. We follow the latter understanding of the temporal aspect of events and consider events to be instantaneous.

Multimedia information systems, however, widen the context of events, as defined in the domain of active databases. In addition to the temporal aspect of an event, which is represented by a *temporal instance*, there are events in IMDs that convey spatial information. This may be represented by a *spatial instance*. For example, an event captures the position of visual objects at a certain point in time. Another aspect that is also crucial in the IMDs context, is that, although the number and multitude of events that are produced both by the user and the system may be huge, we may be interested only in a small subset of them. Thus, events must be treated in a different way in this context, as compared to Active Databases.

We define an event in the context of IMDs as follows:

> *An event is raised by the occurrence of an action and has attached a spatial and temporal instance. The event is recognized by some interested human or process.*

As mentioned in the previous definition, all events have attached to them a temporal instance relative to some reference point, usually the beginning of the IMD. Apart from a temporal instance we assign a spatial instance to an event in case it is related to a visual media object. This spatial instance is essentially the rectangle that bounds an event (e.g., the screen area where the presentation of an image takes place). In some trivial cases though (e.g., mouse click), the rectangle is reduced to a point.

Thus, it is meaningful to integrate the two notions of temporal and spatial instances in the definition of events. Therefore, we introduce the term *spatiotemporal instance* whose representation in tuple form is (sp_inst, temp_inst), where sp_inst is a spatial instance and temp_inst is a temporal instance as defined in sections 2.1 and 2.2, respectively. However, events can be purely temporal, as this is the case for the start event of an audio clip.

2.1.1   Events Classification

In order to assist the authors in the specification of IMDs, we have to provide them with a fundamental *repertoire* of events. In the framework of IMDs we further classify the events into categories. The classification of the events is done on the basis of the entity that produces the event. The elaborated categories are those presented in further sections. This classification forms the basis for the object-oriented modeling, which we propose in section 2.3.2

Events Caused by User Interaction

These are the events that are generated explicitly by user interactions within the IMD context. They are mainly input events as the user interacts with the system via input devices such as mouse, keyboard, touch screen, etc. Such events are:

- *Mouse events* are related to mouse manipulations such as: mouse button clicks, mouse over an object, textline of a list box selected, drag and drop events or scrolling events.

- *Keyboard events* are generated each time a user presses and/or releases a key.

Other input events categories also exist, but they may not be applicable for the moment. However we refer to them for the completeness of the approach. Such events are, for instance, voice input events and events related to touch-screens.

Temporal access control events are the well known actions *start, pause, resume, stop, fast forward, rewind,* and *random positioning in time* and concern the execution of one or a group of media objects. They bear, however, specific semantics for the manipulation of a media object's presentation initiated by the user and this is the reason why we consider them separately in the classification procedure.

Intra-object Events

This category includes events that are related to the internal functionality of an object presented in an IMD. This functionality is implemented in object-oriented approaches as method invocation. For instance, the invocation of a method corresponding to temporal access control such as myObject.start(), produces an intra-object event. Another source of intra-object events is state changes. The viable states of an object as regards its presentation may be temporal (*active, idle, suspended*) and/or spatial (*show, hidden,* and *layer classification* information, etc.). State events occur when there is a state change of a media object, e.g., image I gets hidden, audio A is started, etc. Intra-object events may indicate a discontinuity in the continuous presentation of a media object.

Inter-object Events

Such events occur when two or more objects are involved in the *occurrence of an action of interest*. These events are raised if spatial and/or temporal relationships between two or more objects hold. In the spatial case, an inter-object event can occur if one object, moving spatially, meets another media object. A temporal inter-object event can occur when the deviation between the synchronized presentation of two continuous media objects exceeds a threshold. Moreover, we may consider spatiotemporal inter-media synchronization events. Such events occur, for instance, when two objects are in relative motion during a specified temporal interval (e.g., object A approaches object B before 2am). Although system signals are not classified separately, they can result in inter-object events if, e.g., a low network capacity leads to a video presentation that is too slow (intra-object event) and this raises an inter-object event as the video presentation and an associated audio presentation are not synchronized anymore.

Application Events

In this category we are interested in events related to the IMD *state*. An IMD state bears information that has been contributed essentially by all the objects currently presented in the IMD. Indeed, an IMD as a whole can be *idle, suspended,* or *active.* Moreover, during the execution of an IMD, overall Quality of Service (QoS) parameters is to be taken into consideration [TKWPC96]. Thus, it would be useful if events that indicate a certain state of the IMD were generated. An event indicating that the IMD is idle may lead to an acoustic signal that invites the end user to interact and, thereby, proceed with the IMD. An application event can also indicate that the overall QoP falls below a given (user defined) threshold. For instance, an IMD presents synchronized video and audio data and the network capacity is low. Then, single audio and video presentation generates intra-object events that indicate that their QoP is deteriorating, so as to initiate corresponding actions on the video and the audio presentation. But at the same time it is necessary to have an application event indicating that the overall QoP is going below a certain threshold set. The occurrence of such an event can be paired with a specific action, e.g., only still image is presented instead of the video and present only audio data.

Additionally, timer events may be of interest to denote certain points on the timeline. System signals that indicate the actual system state (such as low network capacity) result in application events that (e.g., indicate that the video presentation is too slow) are not classified separately.

User-Defined Events

In this category we address the events that are defined by the IMD designer. They are related to the content of the IMD execution. A user-defined event can refer to the content of a media object, i.e. to the occurrence of a specific pattern in a media object. For instance, an event is to be raised if the head of a news speaker occurs in a video frame to indicate that the boring advertisements are over and the interesting news are now on.

IMD authors and developers are provided with an initial set of atomic events, namely the ones in the aforementioned categories. In many cases, though, they need to define complex events that are somehow composed of the atomic ones. For instance, assume two atomic events e_1 and e_2 corresponding to the start of video clips A and B, respectively. The video clips are started due to events previously occurred in the IMD. The author might define a composite event e_3 to be raised when e_1 occurred within 3 seconds after e_2 occurred. Another example of a composite event is the occurrence of temporally overlapping presentations of two images img_1 and img_2 between 10:00am and 11:00am. Thus, it is desirable that composite events may be defined by means of a provided set of composition operators. The necessary operators are defined and classified in further sections.

Hereafter we propose an object-oriented modeling approach for events in IMDs, based on the event concept and classification that has been presented above.

2.1.2   Object-Oriented Modeling of Events

An event occurs due to an *action* as defined previously. A subject that may be one or a group of objects participating in the IMD causes this action. If the object is an interaction element, such as a button that has been pressed, the action that caused the event is the user inter-action with the button. Each event occurs at a specific point in time and/or position to which we further refer to as the event's *spatiotemporal signature*. In principle, the event may affect or be related to one or a group of media, further called *object* of the event. Therefore, the modeling of an event must reflect the action that generated the event, its subject and object, as well as its spatiotemporal signature.

In addition to the classification scheme presented in section 2.3.1, we classify events into two layers according to their applicability range. For this second classification, we define the notion of *generic* and *application-specific* events. Generic events are those that convey the semantics of the event, i.e., the action that generated the event. Such a generic event would be the event *Start*, which occurs when a continuous media object presentation is started. However, the event attributes such as spatiotemporal signature, subject and object, are not assigned with values in a generic event. The generic events are the „template" for the IMD definition. The application-specific events are specialization of these generic events. They are defined on the basis of objects belonging to a specific IMD (e.g., the event My_background_music.Start is defined for the media object My_background_music). The IMD scenario designer defines such events during authoring time. They assign the values relevant to the application such as the media object to the event attributes. An initial set of generic events is provided to the authors in order to define the application-specific events, which then serve as the basis for definition of the entire IMD scenario. When the IMD is executed, the application specific events are instantiated, that is, the events actually occur. These *instances* are to be recognized and evaluated by the IMD's execution mechanism. At instantiation time each instance is assigned with its spatiotemporal signature (e.g., My_background_ music.Start (3.5 sec)).

The result of the two classification schemes presented above is a class inheritance tree that is illustrated in Figure 2.1. A related issue is the persistency of generic and application-specific events. It is desirable for many purposes (like reusability, cooperative authoring, consistency, etc.), to have these event classes stored in a database system. Thus, we also gain all the well-known advantages of DBMSs for the storage and management of events. The instances of events, however, are created only at execution time and are not persistent in the database.

Hereafter, we elaborate on the object-oriented specification of the Event class that serves as the root of the hierarchy. First, we define the appropriate data types that are required for the definition of the class. We define data type objectList to represent a list of objects such as media objects, input devices, etc. The data type actionList is needed in order to represent the atomic or complex actions that generated the event. Finally, we need a type spatio_temporal_instance for the representation of spatiotemporal signatures of events as defined before.

According to the aforementioned event definition, we need the following attributes to represent a generic event: The subject and object attributes, that are of type objectList essentially representing the objects that caused or are affected by the event, respectively. The attribute spatio_temporal_signature that takes to the spatial and temporal instances attached to the event when it actually occurs.

Then, the structure of the Event class in an object-oriented pseudo language is as follows:

```
class Event inherits from object
attributes // attribute name              attribute's data type,
     subject                               objectList;
     action                                actionList;
     object                                objectList;
     spatio_temporal_signature  spatiotemp_instance;
end
```

In order to model the inheritance tree illustrated in Figure 2.1, the class Event is specialized by subtyping mechanisms with the respective structure. For instance, a class StateChangeEvent may have additional attributes as new_state, former_state. Subtyping also means that certain values of attributes in subclasses are already set, e.g., the generic event class StartEvent assigns the value start to the action attribute. In this paper, however, we do not elaborate all the definitions of the other generic event classes as they simply specify the aforementioned class description. The generic events are to be persistently stored and managed by a DBMS.

The application-specific events are persistent instances of generic events. The generic events simply offer the structure and behavior of the event types classified in section 2.3.1 to an IMD designer. During the design of an IMD, application-specific events are created to describe the *happenings of interest* to the IMD. The application-specific events hereby assign application-specific values to the attributes of a generic event. For the creation of an application-specific event a generic event is instantiated, assigned to as necessary and persistently stored in the context of an IMD in the database. Only the volatile instances of the application-specific event assign all the remaining attributes with values. For instance, the generic event Start assigns the value start to the action attribute. The corresponding application-specific event My_background_music.Start instantiates an object of class Start and ads the identifier of the medium My_background_music to the subject attribute. During authoring this application-specific event is made persistent. When it comes to the execution of the corresponding IMD, the application-specific event is instantiated. The instances of this event are each assigned values to the remaining attributes, e.g., the spatio_temporal_signature attribute with the values 23.87 sec or 3.5 sec. Figure 2.1 illustrates the described relationships between the persistent generic and application-specific events together with the volatile instances of events during the execution of an IMD.

As we mentioned before, it is important to provide the tools to the authors for the definition of composite events. The composition of events in the context of an IMD has two aspects:

- *Algebraic composition* is the composition of events according to algebraic operators, adapted to the needs and features of an IMD.

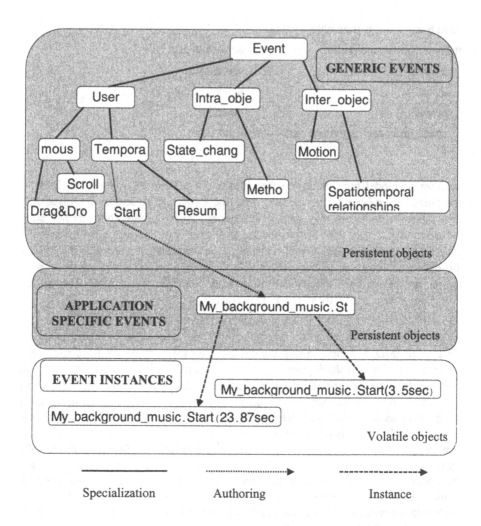

Figure 2.1. Inheritance and instance relationships among events classes in the
         framework of IMDs.

- *Spatiotemporal composition* reflects the spatial and temporal relationships
  between events.

Before explaining these two aspects, we should define some fundamental concepts:

Spatiotemporal reference point (θ):

This is the spatiotemporal start of the IMD scenario named as θ. This serves as the
reference point for every spatiotemporal event and instance in the IMD.

Temporal interval:

This is the temporal distance between two events (e_1, e_2) namely the start and end of
the interval.

t_int :== (e₁,e₂), where e_1, e_2 are events that may either be attached to predefined temporal instances relative to some reference or occur asynchronously.

2.1.3   Algebraic Composition of Events

In many cases the author wants to define specific events that relate to other existing events. We exploited some of the operators presented in other proposals on composite events in Active Databases [G94, GJS92]. We distinguish between the following cases:

Disjunction:

e :== OR($e_1, \ldots, e_n$): This event occurs when at least one of the events $e_1, \ldots, e_n$ occurs. For instance we may be interested in the event e occurring when button A (e_1) or button B (e_2) was pressed.

Conjunction:

e :== ANY(k,$e_1, \ldots, e_n$): This event occurs when at least any k of the events $e_1, \ldots, e_n$ occur. The sequence of occurrence is irrelevant. For example, in an interactive game a user proceeds to the next level when she/he is successful in two out of three tests that generate the corresponding events e_1, e_2, and e_3.

e :== SEQ($e_1, \ldots, e_n$): This event occurs when all events $e_1, \ldots, e_n$ occur in the order appearing in the list. For example, in another interactive game the user proceeds to the next level when she/he succeeds in three tests causing the events e_1, e_2, and e_3 one after the other.

e :== TIMES (n,e_1): This event occurs when there are n consecutive occurrences of event e_1. This implies that other events *may* occur in-between occurrences of e_1.

In many cases the authors want to apply constraints related to event occurrences in specific temporal intervals. To facilitate this requirement we define a set of operators that are of interest in the context of multimedia applications:

Inclusion:

e :== IN(e_1,t_int), event e occurs when event e_1 occurs during the temporal interval t_int. For example, in an IMD we might want to detect three mouse clicks in an interval of 1 sec., so that a help window appears. If t_int = (e_2, e_3), where e_2 corresponds to the starting point of a timer while e_3 corresponds to the end of a timer whose duration is defined as 1 second. The desired event would then be defined as e=IN (TIMES(3,mouse.click), t_int).

Negation:

e :== NOT(e_1,t_int): event e occurs when e_1 does not occur during the temporal interval t_int.

Strictly consecutive events:

In some cases we are interested in whether a series of events of interest is „pure" or mixed up with other events occurring. The event e:== S_CON($e_1, \ldots, e_n$) is raised when all of $e_1,...,e_n$ have occurred in the order appearing in the list and *no other* event occurred in between them.

Apart from the above set of operators we also support the three known boolean operators, namely AND, OR and NOT that have their usual meaning.

2.1.4   Spatiotemporal Composition of Events

In an IMD Session many events may occur. Each of them bears its spatiotemporal signature as described in previous sections. In many cases we are interested to recognize spatiotemporal sequences of events. The term spatiotemporal sequence stands for the spatial and/or temporal ordering of events, e.g., event e1 to occur spatially below and/or temporally after e2.

Temporal Composition of Events

Hereby we discuss the temporal aspect. Since events are of zero temporal duration, the only valid temporal relationships between two events are *after, before,* and *simultaneously.*

Temporal relationship after:

e := after(e_1,e_2), event e occurs when e_1,e_2 have both occurred and the temporal signature of e_1 is smaller than the corresponding signature of e_2.

Temporal relationship before:

e := before(e_1,e_2), event e occurs when e_1,e_2 have both occurred and the temporal signature of e_2 is smaller than the corresponding signature of e_1.

Temporal relationship simultaneously:

e := simultaneously(e_1,e_2), event e occurs when e_1,e_2 have both occurred and the temporal signature of e_1 is equal to the corresponding signature of e_2.

There are cases in which algebraic operators and temporal relationships may be used interchangeably. For instance, for two events e_1,e_2 the expressions after(e_1,e_2) and SEQ(e_1,e_2) convey the same fundamental semantics. Although the former is a temporal relationship between *two* events, the latter is a conjunction operator bearing also temporal semantics for a *list* of events.

Spatial Composition of Events

The spatial aspects are related to position and/or motion of spatial objects (images, buttons etc.). We can assume that each event has a spatial signature that is the rectangle (Minimum Bounding Rectangle) that bounds the area of the event. Spatial relationships between objects involve three different aspects: topology, direction and metrics. A model that represents all these aspects is defined in [VTS96]. We will exploit this model for defining a complete spatiotemporal event composition scheme.

Generic Spatiotemporal Composition Scheme

Having defined all the temporal and spatial relationships among events, we can now introduce a complete spatiotemporal composition scheme. This set of relationships includes the set of all possible spatiotemporal relationships (169 spatial relationships * 3 temporal relationships = 507 spatiotemporal relationships) between two events.

A requirement that arises during event composition specification, is the definition of metrics between events. Thus, we define the notion of *spatiotemporal distance* between two events. For this purpose we consider the definition of the spatial distance between two rectangles as the Euclidean distance between their *closest vertices* as defined in [VTS96]. For our spatiotemporal composition scheme we extend this definition with the temporal distance concept, resulting in the following definition:

Spatiotemporal distance:

Given two events e_1, e_2 having corresponding spatiotemporal signatures: $(x_{11}, y_{11}, x_{12}, y_{12}, t_1)$, $(x_{21}, y_{21}, x_{22}, y_{12}, t_2)$, then the spatiotemporal distance of the two events defined as: spatio_temporal_distance:== $sqrt((x_a - x_b)^2 + (y_a - y_b)^2 + (t_2 - t_1)^2)$, where (x_a, y_a), (x_b, y_b) are the coordinates of the closest vertices of the two spatial distances.

The generic spatiotemporal composition scheme for events, based on the EBNF notation, is defined as follows:

op   :== e_1 Rel e_2

Rel   :== temporal_relation I spatial_relation I sp_temp_dist I boolean_op

temporal_relation   :== "after" I "before" I "simultaneously"

spatial_relation   :== R_{i_j}

i, j   :== [1,13]

spatio_temp_dist   :== spatio_temporal_distance
boolean_op   :== "AND" I "OR" I "NOT"

By having this kind of event composition scheme we gain simplicity, maintain relationships between events, and facilitate queries and playbacks of existing scenaria or simulation of IMDs.

2.2   Spatiotemporal Composition of Media Objects

2.2.1   Basic Concepts

As mentioned in the previous section there is a lack of an integrated approach for representation of all functional aspects of multimedia presentations.   Such an application involves:

- Transformation of objects, in order to be align with the presentation specifications

- Specification of the composition of objects in space and time (spatial and temporal ordering through the definition of relationships among the media objects)

- Definition of the application functionality (i.e., the application scenario) which is of two kinds: *pre-orchestrated*   and *event-based*. The term *pre-orchestrated* implies that certain actions will take place at specific time instants while *event-based* implies that actions are triggered by events that occur in the application context either by the user or the system or by entities participating in the application (media objects, media compositions etc.). The fundamental entities of the scenario are called *scenario tuples* [Vazi96b] and are triggered by the occurrence of an event (simple or complex).

Temporal Relationships

The topic of relations between temporal intervals has been addressed in [Alle83]. In that paper there is a definition of a complete set of 13 temporal relations between two actions. These are *before*, *meets*, *during*, *overlaps*, *starts*, *ends*, *equal* and the inverse ones (does not apply to *equal*). In this section we define a set of concepts to be exploited for representation of temporal composition in the context of an IMD. We consider the execution of a multimedia object as a temporal interval (hereafter *multimedia instance*). We exploit the start- and end- points of a multimedia instance as events and distinguish the end of a multimedia instance in *natural* (i.e., when the media object finishes its execution) and *forced* (i.e., when an event explicitly stops the execution of a media object). Moreover, we are interested in the well-known *pause* (temporarily stop of execution) and *resume* procedures (start the execution from the point where the pause operation took place).

An important concept is the *temporal instance*: we consider it as an arbitrary temporal measurement, relative to some reference point (i.e. the application temporal starting point in our case, hereafter Θ).

Based on the above descriptions we define the following operators attached to the corresponding events:

Definition 1: Let A a multimedia instance, $A>$ represents the start of the multimedia instance, $A<$ the natural end of the instance, $A!$ the forced stop, $A||$ the pause and $A|>$ the resume actions respectively.

Definition 2: Let A, B two multimedia instances, then the expression $Aop1$ t $Bop2$ represents all temporal relationships between the two multimedia instances, where $op1 \in \{>,<,||,|>\}$ and $op2 \in \{>,!,||,|>\}$ and t is a vacant temporal interval.

Definition 3: Let A be a multimedia instance, we define as t_{Aop} temporal instances corresponding to the events Aop, where $Aop \in \{>,<,!,||,|>\}$.

Definition 4: Let A be multimedia instance, we define as d_A the temporal duration of the multimedia instance A.

The above operators are complete in the sense that all temporal relationships can be expressed using these operators as long as the appropriate conditions are fulfilled (Figure 2.2). Additionally the proposed operators capture the semantics of the temporal relationships among the multimedia instances (i.e. A meets B may be expressed as A< 0 B> or B>0 A!). Moreover, the proposed set of operators may be used for a high level mechanism of temporal scenario specification.

Temporal Relationship		Equivalent operator expression	Conditions
A before B	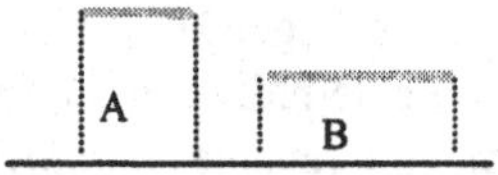	A <t B>	
A meets B	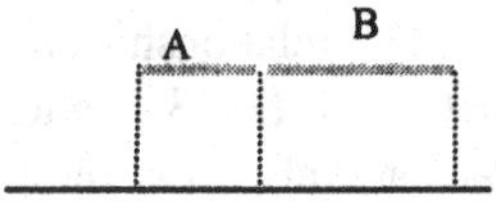	A< 0 B>	
A during B	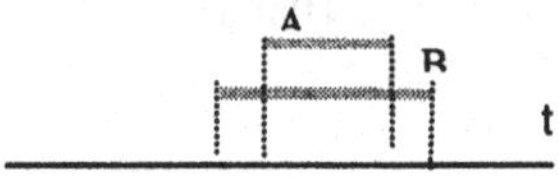	A >t B>	$t+d_A<d_B$
A overlaps B	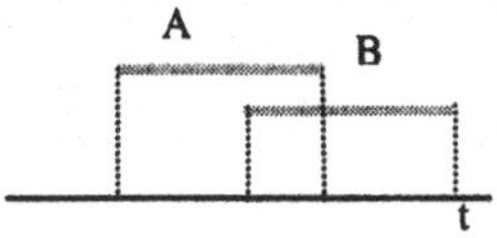	A >t B>	$t<d_A$
A ends B	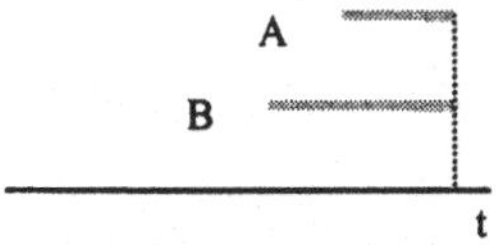	A< 0 B!	
A starts B	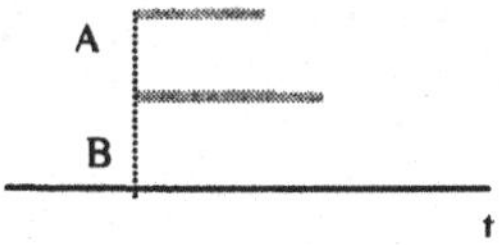	A> 0 B>	
A equal B	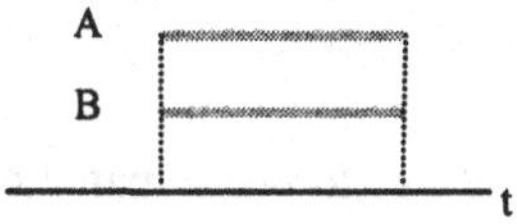	A> 0 B>	$d_A = d_B$

Figure 2.2. Temporal relationships and the corresponding operator expressions

Spatial Relationships

Another aspect of composition regards the spatial ordering and topological features of the participating objects. Spatial composition aims at representing three aspects:

- The topological relationships between the objects (*disjoint*, *meet*, *overlap* etc.)

- The directional relationships between the objects (*left*, *right*, *above*, *above-left* etc.)

- The distance characteristics between the objects (*outside* 5cm, *inside* 2cm etc.)

As for the first aspect, a complete set of topological relationships between two objects, called *4-intersection model*, was proposed in [Egen91]. Thus two objects *p*, *q* may coincide (*equal*), intersect (*overlap*), touch externally (*meet*), touch internally (*covers* and the reverse *covered_by*), be *inside* (and the reverse *contains*), or be *disjoint*.

As for the directional relationships, there is a complete set of relationships defined in [Papa97] (see Figure 2.3). This set of 169 (13^2) relationships R_{i_j} ($i = 1, ..., 13$ and $j = 1, ..., 13$) arises from exhaustive combination of the 13 relations defined in [Alle83] regarding relationships between temporal intervals. This set also covers topological relationships, since any topological relationship of the 4-intersection model, could be expressed as a subset of the set of 169 relationships [Papa95].

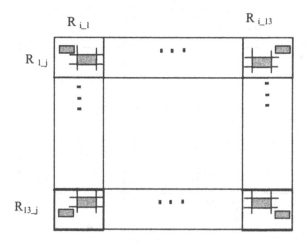

Figure 2.3. Directional relationships between two spatial objects   (including topological information)

In the context of an IMD an author would like to place spatial objects (text windows, images, video clips, animation) in the application window in such a way that their relationships are clearly defined in a declarative way, i.e., *"text window A is placed at the location (100, 100), text window B appears 8cm to the right and 12cm below the upper side of A"* (see its illustration Figure 2.4). This declarative definition should be transformed in an internal representation that captures the topological and directional relationships as well as the distance between the objects in a uniform and correct way. In the next subsection we propose a definition model to support these needs.

2.2.2   Spatiotemporal Composition Model

Current IMD modeling schemes do not provide powerful tools for the complete description of the spatial and temporal composition that takes place in a complex application (an overview of related work was presented in Section 2).

We define a set of operators for representing temporal and spatial composition. Here we have to make the distinction between pre-orchestrated and interactive applications. The term *"pre-orchestrated"* implies that certain actions will take place at specific time and/or spatial instants (i.e. temporal location relative to the applications start or spatial location in the application window) while *"event-based"* implies that actions are triggered by events that occur in the application context either by the user or the system or by entities participating in the application (media objects, media compositions etc.)

The resulting requirement is for a set of operators that allows users to represent any spatiotemporal relationship between objects in the context of an IMD in a declarative way. As for temporal composition of objects we exploit the operators defined above. As far as it concerns spatial composition we are based on the complete set of topological-directional relationships illustrated in Figure 2.3, and propose the following generalized methodology for representing the distance between two spatial objects[1]. For having a uniform approach we impose the constraint that the distance will be expressed in terms of distance between the "closest vertices". For each spatial object O we label its vertices as $O.v_i$ ($i = 1, 2, 3, 4$) starting clock-wise from the bottom left vertex. As "closest" we define the pair of vertices ($A.v_i$, $B.v_j$) having the minimum Euclidean distance, $dist(A.v_i, B.v_j)$, which, in general, is defined as follows:

$$dist(p_i, q_j) = \sqrt{\left(p_{i\_x} - q_{j\_x}\right)^2 + \left(p_{i\_y} - q_{j\_y}\right)^2}$$

The author of an IMD must be able to express spatial composition predicates in an unlimited manner. For instance (see Figure 2.4), the author could describe the appearing composition as *"object B to appear 12cm lower that the upper side of object A and 8cm to the right"*. The model we propose will translate such descriptions into minimal and uniform expressions as imposed by the requirements for correct and complete representations.

---

[1] We assume that spatial objects are rectangles. More complex objects can also be represented as rectangles by using their Minimum Bounding Rectangle (MBR) approximation.

For uniformity reasons we define an object named Θ, that corresponds to the spatial and temporal start of the application (i.e., the upper left corner of the application window and the temporal start of the application). Another assumption we make is that the objects that appear in the composition include their spatiotemporal presentation characteristics (i.e. size, temporal duration etc.) [Vazi95].

In the following we exploit the EBNF formalism to represent the model primitives.

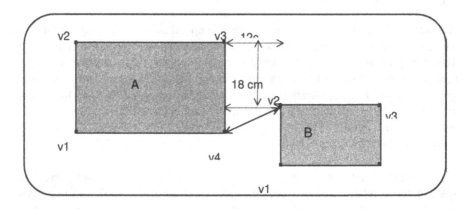

Figure 2.4. Spatial composition generalised modelling.

Definition 1: Assuming two spatial objects A, B, we define the generalized spatial relationship between these objects as: S_R = (r_{ij}, v_i, v_j, x, y) where r_{ij} is the identifier of the topological-directional relationship between A and B, v_i, v_j are the closest vertices of A and B respectively and x, y are the horizontal and vertical distances between v_i, vj.

Now we need to define a generalized operator expression to cover the spatial and temporal relationships between objects in the context of an IMD. It is important to stress the fact that in some cases we do not need to model a relationship between two objects but to declare the spatial and / or temporal position of an object relative to the application spatial and temporal start point Θ (i.e., object A to appear at the spatial coordinates (110, 200) on the 10th second of the application).

Definition 2: We define a composite spatiotemporal operator that represents absolute spatial/temporal coordinates or spatiotemporal relationships between objects in the application: ST_R(sp_rel, temp_rel), where sp_rel is a spatial relationship (S_R) while temp_rel is a temporal relationship as defined in section 3.1.

The spatiotemporal composition of an IMD consists of several independent fundamental compositions. The term "independent" implies that objects participating in them are not related implicitly (either spatially or temporally) except from their implicit relationship to the start point Θ. Thus all compositions are explicitly related to Θ. We call these compositions *composition_tuples* and these include spatially and/or temporally related objects.

Definition 3. We define the composition_tuple in the context of an IMD as: composition_tuple = Ai [{ ST_R Aj}], where Ai, Aj are objects participating in the application, ST_R is a spatiotemporal relationship (as defined in definition 2).

Definition 4. We define the composition of multimedia objects in the context of IMDs as a set of composition_tuples: composition = Ci {, Cj}, where Ci, Cj are composition_tuples.

The EBNF definition of the spatiotemporal composition based on the above definition follows:

composition ==:	composition_tuple{[,composition_tuple]}
composition_tuple ==:	Θ {[spatio_temporal_relationship action]}
action ==:	object [{spatio_temporal_relationship object}]
I	"(" object spatio_temporal_relationship object ")"
I	object
I	spatio_temporal_instance
spatio_temporal_relationship ==:	
	"[("[spatial_operator I spatial_instance")",
	"("temporal_operator I temporal_instance")]"
temporal_operator ==:	Θ I t_event t_interval TAC_operation
t_event ==:	">" I "<" I "!" I "I>" I "II"
TAC_operation ==:	">"I"!"I"I>"I"II"
spatio_temporal_instance ==:	Θ I (spatial_instance, temporal_instance)
spatial_instance ==:	"("x "," y ")"
temporal_instance ==:	TIME I event
spatial_operator ==:	(rij, Vi, Vj, x, y)
x ==:	INTEGER
y ==:	INTEGER
Θ ==:	application start :(0,0,0)

where rij denotes a topological- directional relationship between two objects and vi, vj denote the closest vertices of the two objects (see definition above).

In this section we proposed a model for representing spatiotemporal composition in pre-orchestrated IMDs. In the next subsection we illustrate the potential of the model through a sample application.

2.3   Interactive Scenario Modeling

The term scenario in the context of IMDs stands for the integrated behavioral contents of the IMD, i.e. what kind of events the IMD will consume and what actions will be triggered as a result. The scenario, in the current approach, consists of a set of autonomous functional units (*scenario tuples*) that include the triggering events (for starting and stopping the scenario tuple), the presentation actions to be carried out in the context for the scenario tuple, related synchronization events and possible constraints. Initial efforts for definition of scenario tuples may also be found in [VM93, VS96]. More specifically a scenario tuple has the following attributes:

- Start_event: represents the event expression that triggers the execution of the actions described in the Action_list.

- Stop_event: represents the event expression that terminates the execution of this tuple (i.e. the execution of the actions described in the Action_List before its expected termination.

- Action_List: represents the list of synchronized media presentation actions that will take place when this scenario tuple becomes activated. The expressions included in this attribute are in terms of compositions as described in previous sections and as in [VTS96].

- Synch_events: refers to the events generated (if any) at the beginning and at the end of the current tuple execution. These events may be used for synchronization purposes.

The scenario tuple may be defined as follows:

scenario:==	scenario_tuple [{,scenario_tuple}]
scenario_tuple :==	Start_event ',' Stop_event ',' Action_List ',' Synch_events
Start_event :==	Event
Stop_event :==	Event
Action_List :==	composition
Synch_events :==	'(' start, end ')'
start :==	string
stop :==	string

We present a sample IMD scenario with rich interaction and composition features. One of the parts of the scenario should adhere to the following verbal description:

"The next set of media presentations ("Stage 2B") is initiated when the sequence of events _IntroStop and _ACDSoundStop occurs. During Stage2b the video clip KAVALAR starts playback while the buttons NEXTBTN and EXITBTN are presented. The presentation actions are interrupted when any of the events _TIMEINST and _NextBtnClick occurs. The end of Stage2b raises the synchronization event _e1."

The IMD scenario model may represent this functionality by the following scenario tuple definition:

TUPLE Stage2B

        Start Event = SEQ(_IntroStop;_ACDSoundStop)

        Stop Event = ANYNEW(1;_TIMEINST;_NextBtnClick)

        Action List = KAVALAR> 0 NEXTBTN> 0 EXITBTN>

        Start Synch Event = None

        Stop Synch Event = _e1

In the following sections we use interchangeably the terms "composition tuple" and "instruction stream".

3. Authoring Interactive Multimedia Presentations

Creating multimedia/hypermedia documents requires two major steps: authoring and publishing. If we use the creation of a paper book as an analogy, then this first step is the creation of authoring of the underlying information (words, story, plot, themes, etc.) This information them needs to be published (typeset printed, bound etc.). It is viable to say that multimedia documents go through a similar process. Authoring is the process of creating and storing information in a fashion appropriate to its intended uses. This often involves either transforming existing information sources or creating new information to populate an information repository. Publishing is the process of of presenting this information to the user, including issues such as look and feel, screen layout and usability.

The term *authoring* has often been used to refer to the entire multimedia document creation process, including publishing.

In this section an implemented authoring system is presented. The system is based on the IMD model presented in previous chapters and the authoring procedure is carried out in three consecutive phases corresponding to the basic modeling primitives. The IMD author may move in an iterative way between these three phases. The authoring phases are clearly distinguished and are the following:

- Selection and transformation of the media objects to participate; the author selects the media objects to participate in the IMD and defines the spatial and temporal transformations of the objects in the context of the current IMD.

- Definition of the events (atomic and complex) that the IMD session will consume; the author defines the atomic events that the current IMD will exploit for the scenario.

- Specification of the scenario of the IMD session in terms of scenario tuples. The scenario consists of autonomous units (scenario tuples as defined in previous sections), which consist of the event expression that if occurs activates the tuple, and the expression that if occurs de-activates the tuple prior to its expected end. The media objects to be presented in a synchronized way (in space and time) are included in the Actions List attribute of the scenario tuple.

The authoring process is an iterative loop between the aforementioned phases. The authors may refine/redefine their design and produce the desired IMD functionality. The relationships among the authoring phases are depicted in Figure 3.1.

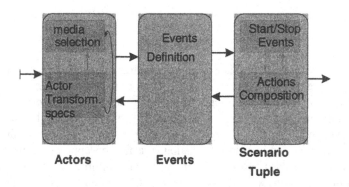

Figure 3.1. The authoring phases and their relationships.

The result of the first phase is a set of objects (*actors*) that represent the objects that will participate in the IMD along with their spatiotemporal transformations. This set of actors are exploited in the second phase, in order to define events related to/ generated by them. In the next phase the actors and events are inter-related in order to form the scenario of the application. We will elaborate on the authoring procedure phases in the following sections.

3.1   Actor Specifications and Transformations

The objective of this phase is the selection of the media objects to participate in the IMD as well as their spatiotemporal features and transformations in order to align to the authors requirements. In this phase (step 1 of 3, see Figure 3.2) the author selects the media objects to participate in the IMD. This is carried our by selecting the "Add" button. Pressing the "Preview" button the author may preview (view an image, play a sound or a video) the object under concern. At this point the author is able to transform the object for the purposes of the current IMD

These transformations are related to the object's spatial and temporal features (see Figure 3.3). The author may define the logical name of the actor ("Actor_id"), the corresponding media file and the path in which it resides. With regards to the spatial features, the author may define the position of the actor in the application window ("Xcoord", and "Ycoord" coordinates of the upper left corner of the media objects relative to the upper left corner of the application window), and the size of the object ("Height" and "Width") in terms of screen units. As for the temporal features (which applies in the case of time-dependent media objects like sound and video) the author

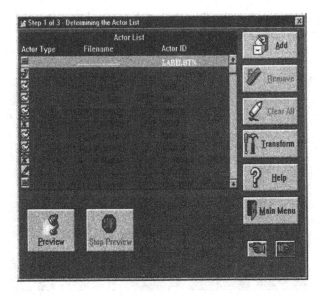

Figure 3.2. Definition of an actor with both spatial and temporal features

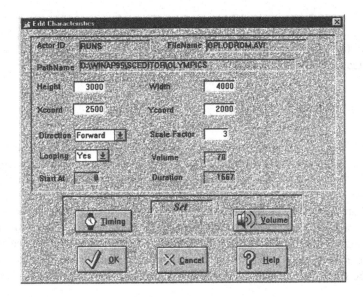

Figure 3.3. Definition of an actor with both spatial and temporal features

may define: the playback direction, the temporal portion of the object to participate in the application ("Start At" and "Duration" attributes) and the playback speed ("Scale" factor, essentially the temporal scaling). More refined control over the second feature may be achieved through the "Timing" button leading to the dialog box of Figure 3.4.

In this dialog box the user may select the exact temporal portion of the media object under concern while previewing it (either video or audio clip).

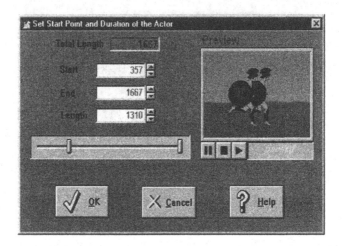

Figure 3.4. Temporal actor length definition

The actors have already been selected and properly defined with all their presentation features. The next step would be the definition of the events that our IMD will be "interested in" and will consume upon their occurrence.

3.2   Event Specification

The IMD may be considered as a context where events occur and are consumed according to the interest of the IMD. The authors may want to define happenings that are of interest to the IMD in order to trigger presentation actions. The authoring system provides a flexible event definition framework based on the model defined in [VB97] and presented in previous sections. The author may define a new event in terms of its *subject* (i.e. the actor that generates the event) and action (i.e. the action(s) of the actor that generates the event). The related dialog box is presented in Figure 3.5. There the event "_TIMEINST" is defined and raised when the actor TIMER1 counts 50 sec. In this stage only simple (atomic) events may be defined.

In Figure 3.5, the event specification process is depicted. The user provides a name for the current event. The event is checked in the IMD context for uniqueness (as for its name) and, then, the author may select one of the actors (defined in the previous phase) as the subject of the event (i.e. the object that generates the event). Depending on the type of the actor (time-dependent, button, timer etc.) there is a different repertoire of actions available that may be selected at the "Action" dropdown list. Apart from the IMD specific media actors, there are some objects available to all IMDs (the corresponding repertoire of actions appear in brackets): Application Timer (time instance, started at, Application start), System Settings (time, date), Keyboard (a set of keys like "Enter", "Esc" etc.) and Mouse ("Left Button Click", "Double Click" etc.). The user may select the "Action" that will generate the event under concern. For each different object type that the user selects as the subject of the event there is a different repertoire of events that are available for this object. For instance if the subject of the event is a video object then the available actions are: *start, stop, pause, resume, fast forward, rewind.*

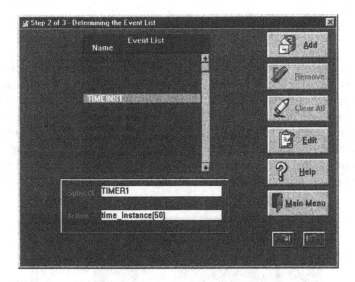

Figure 3.5. Definition of the atomic events that will be consumed in the application

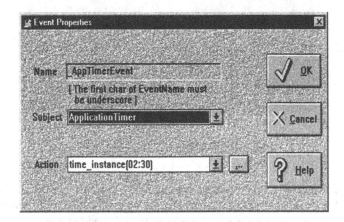

Figure 3.6. Editing the event properties.

Thus, the definition of events may be carried out in terms of the steps described above.

Then, the scenario of the IMD may be defined. As scenario we perceive the behavioral contents of the IMD, i.e. what presentation actions will take place in the IMD context and how the IMD will respond to external (user, system) or internal (IMD actors) interaction. This is the objective of the third authoring phase described in the next section.

3.3   Scenario Tuples Specifications

The term scenario in the context of IMDs stands for the integrated behavioral contents of the IMD, i.e. what kind of events the IMD will consume and what actions will be triggered as a result. The scenario, in the current approach, consists of a set of autonomous functional units (*scenario tuples*) that include the triggering events, the presentation actions to be carried out in the context for the scenario tuple, related synchronization events and possible constraints. The scenario tuple specification process that will be described hereafter is based on the model presented in [VM93, VS96] and also in previous sections.

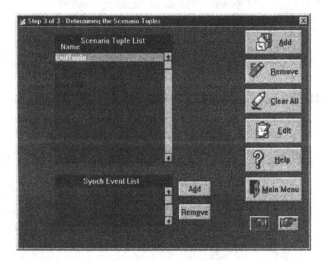

Figure 3.7. Definition of scenario tuples

The user interface for scenario tuples manipulation appears in Figure 3.7. At this point, the list of already defined tuples and the sync_events (i.e. the events that are raised when the scenario tuple starts / ends) of the selected tuple appear. The detailed scenario definition tuple procedure appears in Figure 3.8. There the user may provide the name of the scenario tuple (which must be unique in the IMD context), then the "Start Event" and "Stop Event" may be defined.

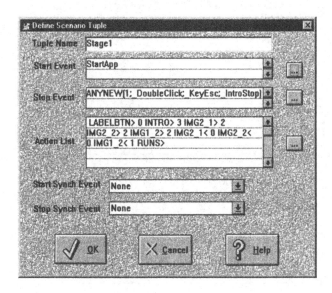

Figure 3.8. The attributes of a scenario tuple.

The dialog box appearing in Figure 3.9 facilitates this purpose. At that point the author may define an arbitrarily complex event expression using the available composition functions and operators defined in earlier sections and presented in detail in [VB97]. The complex event consists of one or more expressions separated by brackets. The user interface forces syntactic correctness since the user may only select terms and adds them to the event expression rather than typing free text. During event definition, syntactic checking is done and errors are reported before leaving the Start/Stop event definition procedure. The user may edit each bracket separately.

The next step would be the definition of the actions that will be triggered by the activation of the scenario tuple. The actions are essentially an expression that includes synchronized presentation actions of the IMD actors. The temporal ordering and the relationships between the presentations actions are defined in terms of the temporal composition operators set defined in [VTS98] and presented in previous sections. The author selects an actor from the "Actor list" (see Figure 3.10). Then the available set of Operators for the selected actor types appear in the "Operators" list and the author may select any of them. The author may as well add the temporal interval between two actor operators, whenever applicable. The action expression is again organized in independent expressions, enclosed in brackets, that are conjunctive and their contents are simultaneously triggered upon tuple activation.

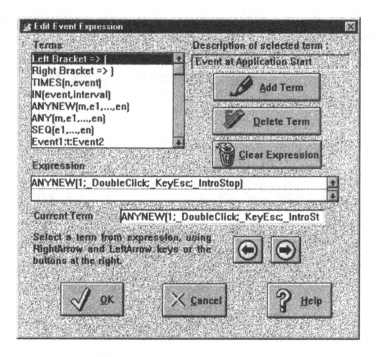

Figure 3.9. Editing the event expression for start and stop events

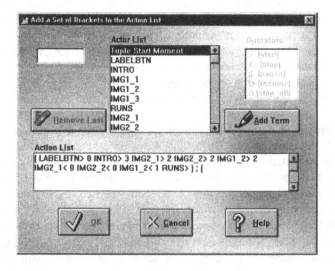

Figure 3.10. Adding action expressions in the "Action List"attribute of the scenario
tuple.

It is important to stress the syntactic check that takes place before leaving this stage. Any errors are reported and the user is prompted to fix them.

The editing procedure of each bracket is carried out separately; the related user interface appears in Figure 3.11. At that point the user may select the actors to be presented (from the "Actors" list), the order of presentation ("Actor Position"), the temporal relationships among these presentations (from the "Operators" list) and the involved temporal interval length ("Time Interval").

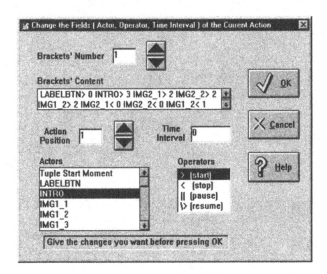

Figure 3.11. Editing an action expression in the action attribute of the scenario tuple.

The result of the above authoring process is a declarative script. Such script appears in the sample application in APPENDIX A. This script needs to be transformed into algorithms in order to be exploited for building the IMD executable version. This transformation is described in the following chapter.

4. Spatiotemporal Specification & Verification for Multimedia Scenarios

An IMD involves a variety of individual media objects, referred to as *actors*, presented according to the scenario. The term *scenario* covers two areas: i. the spatial and temporal ordering of actors within the application context and the relationships among them and ii. the way that the user will interact with the application as well as how the application will treat application or system events.

Another relevant issue is that the actors participating in an IMD, are transformed either spatially and/or temporally in order to be presented according to the author's requirements. For instance we may want to present part of a video clip faster or slower at a bigger or smaller window.

The authoring procedure for complex IMDs, that involve a large number of actors, may be a very complicated task, having in mind the large set of possible events that may be encountered in the application context, the number of actors and relationships as well as the various potential combinations of these factors.

An IMD specification should describe both the temporal and spatial ordering of actors in the context of the IMD. In the past, the term "synchronization" has been widely used to describe the temporal ordering of actors in an IMD. The spatial ordering issues (i.e. absolute position and spatial relationships among actors) have not adequately been addressed up to now. We claim that the term synchronization is poor for IMDs. Instead we propose the term "*composition*" to represent both the temporal and the spatial composition of actors.

The potential high complexity of IMDs, results in substantial effort required for design and development. In real-life applications, usually only programmers are able to develop IMD scenarios since current authoring tools provide rather low level specification languages. Moreover, these languages are inadequate for the complete description of the scenario aspects mentioned before. Therefore, the lack of an integrated mechanism for high level complete specification of an IMD scenario arises as a main issue. Moreover, in current IMD authoring tools the IMD script is mixed with the application content (actors). This prevents the explicit reusability of scenarios in other IMDs with different content but similar functionality.

Another important aspect is the verification of IMD scenarios during IMD authoring. The term verification in this context implies the various procedures that will allow the author to review the result of their authoring effort prior to the production and execution of the IMD. This will enable revisiting the application and adjusting the spatiotemporal specification in order to align to the document style the authors has in mind or to fix specification errors that result in spatial and or temporal exceptions.

In Figure 4.1 we can see the IMD development procedures in terms of modules as described earlier. We can see the two distinct main phases namely the specification and the verification phase. In the first the author specify the transformation of the original multimedia objects in order to participate in the IMD while in the second the author may verify several aspects of the IMD by obtaining spatial and temporal layouts or by viewing an animation of the IMD prior to the execution time.

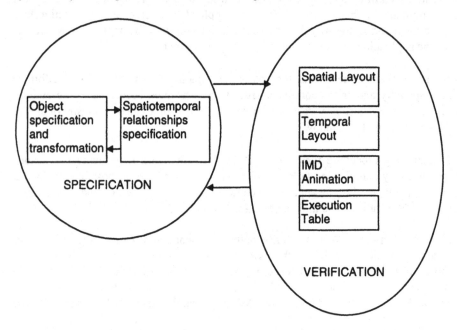

Figure 4.1. The authoring & verification cycle for an IMD.

In this chapter we present an authoring & verification methodology for IMD documents development supported by a full implementation. The IMD design is based on a theoretical model for spatiotemporal compositions in the context of multimedia presentations [Vaz98]. The tool may be used both for *prototyping* and *verification* of multimedia presentations or spatiotemporal compositions in general.

Regarding the authoring phase, emphasis was put on the flexible definition of spatial and temporal relationships of the participating entities. In other words, the authoring phase consists mainly of declarative specifications of the spatial and temporal ordering of participating multimedia objects based on their spatial and temporal relationships.

The *verification* procedures are supported by multiple tools allowing designers to preview their applications, in various ways: *spatial layouts* of the application window, *temporal layout* of parts (or the whole application), indicating the temporal duration and relationships among the participating objects and *animation (rendering)* of the application (i.e. what would the execution of the application like) in three modes (real time, manual and snapshots of the application at regular temporal intervals).

The chapter is organized as follows. In the next section we present the authoring procedures as spatiotemporal specification of multimedia objects and in section three we present the verification tools provided by the system. In the last section, we conclude by presenting our contributions and discussing on further research and extensions of the tool.

4.1   Authoring Spatiotemporal Compositions for IMD Documents

The authoring methodology we present hereafter is based on the model introduced in previous in chapter two. An IMD document contains objects composed in space and time according to a set of spatial and temporal relationships. The scenario is build in a stepwise procedure. The first step is the specification of the objects that participate in the application along with their spatial and temporal transformations (i.e. which spatial and/or temporal part of the object will participate in the IMD, under what spatial/temporal scaling etc.). The second step is to define the actors' spatial and temporal position in the IMD document in terms of absolute or relative coordinates. The authoring tool transforms these specifications and produces the spatiotemporal scenario, i.e. when, where and for how long each object will be presented.

We distinguish the actors in four main categories: text, sound, image and video. We assume that each object (except sound) has some spatial extent so it can be represented by a rectangle in which the image text/video information is presented. The sound objects on the other hand have only temporal aspects.

4.1.1   Authoring Environment

The authoring interface supports to a great extend visual definition of the multimedia scenario. Conceptually the scenario specification should start at the temporal start of the IMD. Thus, the authoring procedure starts at the beginning of the application (time = 0) and specifies the participating actors in a more or less increasing temporal order. Figure 4.2 gives an overview of the working environment.

Composition Specifications

Initially the author may insert or remove media objects from the actors list. Each actor object is further defined by assigning values to its spatial and temporal attributes.

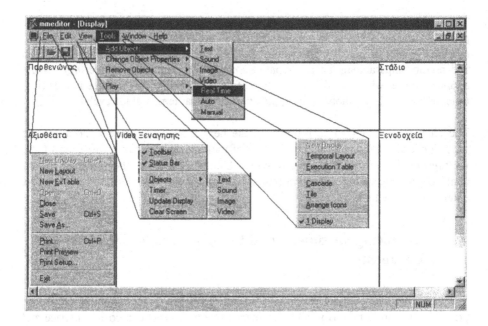

Figure 4.2. The authoring environment menu options.

Each actor includes its identification data such as name, media type and media file corresponding to the actor (see Figure 4.3), the temporal and spatial coordinates of the object in the application context. The name of an actor must be unique in the IMD context. Though the tool allows for the definition of different actors based on the same media object. The data that the user enters (*external*), are transformed into absolute coordinates (*internal*) in order to produce the spatiotemporal specifications of the scenario. The external data mostly relate the spatial and temporal coordinates of the new object to those of other objects, previously defined.

The methodology supports incremental authoring by adding new actors to the existing spatiotemporal composition and relating it to them spatially and/or temporally.

Temporal attributes specification

The *temporal attributes* of the object include its temporal start and end points (see Figure 4.4). Thus the start time is related to the temporal application origin Θ, or to the start/end point of another object. More specifically the author may define the start point of the actor under concern to be a number of time units after Θ or a number of time units before/after the start/end point of another actor. The same applies to the definition of the *end* time of the object as long as it does not have a predefined temporal duration (like video and sound objects). As it is widely known there is a

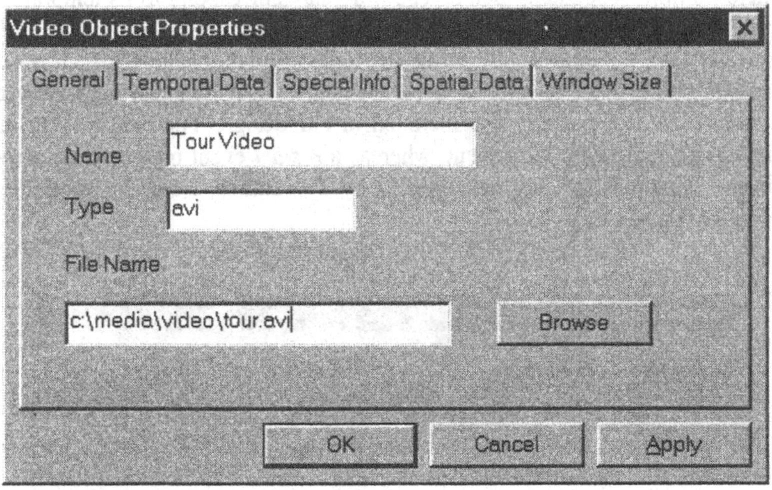

Figure 4.3. Specification of general attributes of an actor

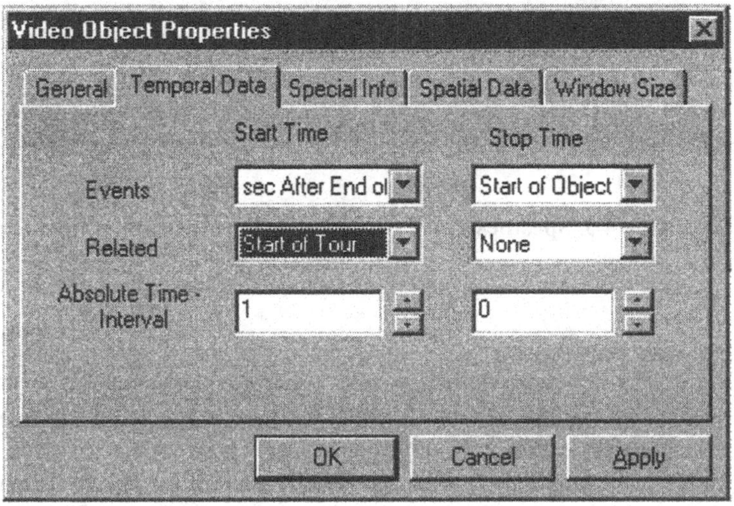

Figure 4.4. The Properties of an object to participate in the IMD (temporal data).

fundamental set of temporal access control actions (see chapter two) to control the presentation of a temporal object: *start, pause, resume* and *stop*. The start time as we define it in the spatiotemporal compositions may either be generated by the *start* or the *restart* action. In a similar way the stop time is related to either a stop or a pause event. These choices may be done by the author (see Figure 4.5).

If the actor is time dependent, then its end time may correspond to its temporal length or it can be forced to stop before that. That event can be a stop or a pause event. As mentioned before, the author may define the temporal data of the actor in relation to the starting/ending point of another actor. We have to distinguish here between the events *pause, restart* that are also included in our design. The *pause* event may be considered as a temporary *stop* event, whereas a *restart* event may be considered as a *start* event. This setting may be adjusted by the author using the property sheet appearing in Figure 4.4.

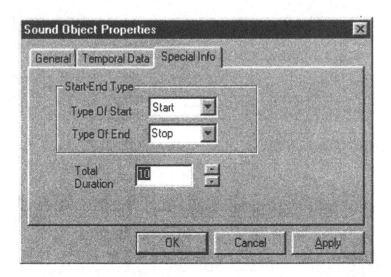

Figure 4.5. Specification of the start and stop events of an actor

Spatial attributes specification

The issue of spatial features of actors in IMDs has been rather under-addressed in the multimedia literature. Only recently there have been some research efforts [Iin94][Vaz98]. The authoring tools enable specification of the spatial features of an actor, either as absolute coordinates or in relation to other objects. We assume that each object is bounded by a rectangle (whose dimensions may be changed by the author) and the author may define its position. The actor's upper left corner is related by a spatial distance either to the origin of the IMD (Θ) or to any vertice (Upper Left, Upper Right, Lower Left, Lower Right) of any other actor already defined. It is important to stress that it is possible to relate the actor under concern to different actors regarding the X and Y axis. In the case of absolute coordinates we define the position of the upper left corner of the actor, related to the top left corner of the application window (see Figure 4.6).

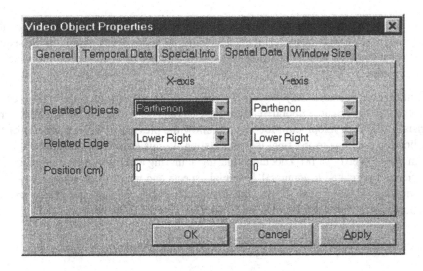

Figure 4.6. The spatial properties of an actor.

4.2   Verification of IMD Documents

During the authoring procedure it is anticipated that the author might want to query the scenario, especially if it is extended and complicated in terms of interactions and composed presentation actions. This can be helpful in order to:

- Inform the author about the underlying spatiotemporal constraints of the scenario,
- Modify the scenario and, in this way, create, correct or improve the scenario in an incremental way.

In this last case, the author, depending on the answer of the query, can do the modification on the scenario, currently under creation. The queries may be classified into the following categories:

- *Point queries*, which queries are useful when the author is interested in finding relationships between events. For instance: "Does actor Starting Logo start before Tour video?" or "which objects appear at the position (50,50) before the 5th second of the IMD"?

- *Relationship queries*: In this category we are interested in relationships among the temporal intervals that represent the presentations of actors [All83] or alternatively the relationships between the spatial extents of the actors. Such a queries would be: "Are the presentations of objects "tour_video" and "agora"simultaneous?" or "Is "tour_video" overlapping with "agora"?".

- *Layout queries*. Such queries result in graphical representations, depicting the spatial and temporal relationships among presented objects. Such kind of queries is a necessity that is recognized among the authoring community [Vaz98]. An example can be: "Show the temporal layout of the IMD between the 2nd and 10th second of the presentation".

It is evident that handling such queries can enhance the flexibility and quality of the authoring procedure through verification of the IMD under development. In the sequel we present the tools and methodologies we have developed to tackle the above set of requirements.

A multimedia scenario may be very complicated if we consider the multitude of objects and the spatiotemporal relationships among them. Thus it is essential for a consistent IMD development procedure to allow the preview of several aspects of the application previous to the final implementation. In this section we introduce a set of techniques to verify an IMD document during authoring and prior to its execution. The verification is related to temporal & spatial aspects and may fulfill requirements such as viewing IMD snapshots at any temporal point, finding out the temporal relationships between actors, viewing an animation of the IMD etc.

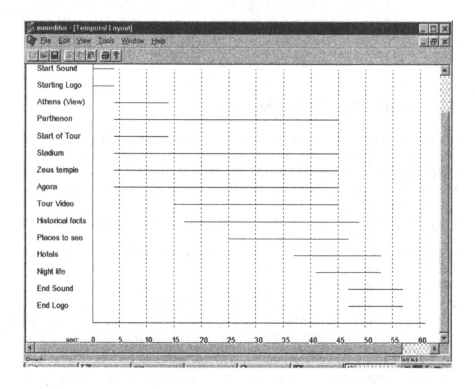

Figure 4.7. The temporal layout of the IMD

4.2.1   Temporal Layout Tool

The first verification tool is the *temporal layout* that displays, in a graphical form, the temporal order and the duration of the actors (see Figure 4.7). This facility gives an overview of the temporal configuration of the IMD and moreover provides support to queries of the type: "which objects are active at a specific time?" or "which objects are active at a specific period of time?" (i.e. during the temporal interval in which another object is active). The temporal layout may refer to a part of the temporal duration of the IMD (e.g. from the 5th to the 20th second of the IMD) or to its total duration. The list of objects (in absolute temporal coordinates) is sorted according to their starting time. This list is exploited in the rest of the verification tools, more specifically in the execution table and in the spatial layout tool that are described hereafter.

4.2.2   Spatial Layout

The term "spatial layout" implies the appearance of the IMD application window, conveying information about the position and dimensions of the actors participating in the IMD. It is important for IMD authors to be able to preview the IMD Spatiotemporal layout at any time during the development, so the appropriate modification may take place. The spatial layout tool makes possible for the author to view how the application window will look like at any temporal point during a potential IMD execution (e.g. which objects and where on the application window, appear on the 20th sec. of the IMD). The temporal duration of each object is derived from the temporal layout.

The author may set the desired time point (see Figure 4.8) in the *timer* dialog box and then with *update display* option get the layout of the screen. Thus the display may be checked before a new object is inserted and find *if* and *where* it should be placed.

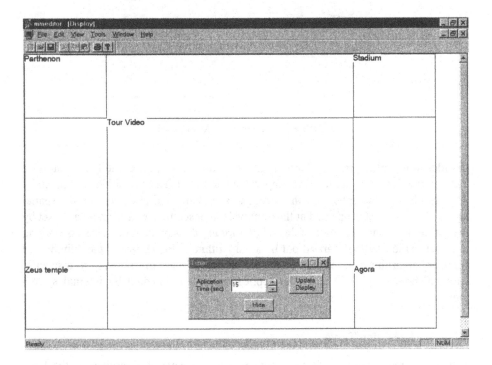

Figure 4.8. The spatial layout of the IMD at any time using the "Timer" tool.

4.2.3   Scenario Animation Tool

The most appealing feature of the verification tool is the opportunity to render (animate) the application, in other words to have an animated view of the spatiotemporal specifications of an IMD, in terms of spatial snapshots of the IMD evolving through time. This is accomplished through the "play" tool (see Figure 4.9). In this chapter we use the terms "rendering" and "animation" interchangeably. The animation is a simulation of an IMD execution session using consecutive snapshots of the application updated at regular time intervals. The author may change the value of this interval. The default temporal granularity is one second. This kind of animation enables the author notice any mistakes or misplacements and to mend them later.

The author has the opportunity to change the time limits of the animation and animate only a temporal part of the IMD (i.e. for the 5th to the 25th second). The animation may be interrupted at any time, changes in the scenario may be done and then resume again into animation to verify the changes. The default values of the time limits (see Figure 4.9) are: 0 (for "Start Time") and the last second of the IMD (for the "End Time").

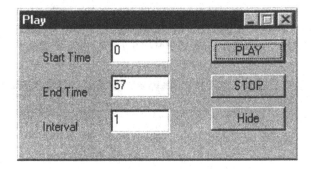

Figure 4.9. Scenario rendering tool.

In order to be able to manage large numbers of actors, we exploit the functionality of the previous tools (the spatial and temporal layout tools). The animation is initiated by a list of objects that appear on the screen at start time, and is created by the spatial layout tool. This list is updated at time intervals imposed by the time granularity set by the author using the execution table and performing the actions it describes. Searching in the execution table is carried out by an algorithm of the family of the "divide and conquer" algorithms, in order to locate the actions of the corresponding to a specific temporal point (e.g. 10th sec). The application time is handled by internal system timers.

4.2.4   Execution Table

A common requirement is that the authors need to have an overview of the IMD structure in ascending temporal order. This need is fulfilled by the execution table tool.

This table, that may be generated at any time during the authoring session, includes the temporal and spatial coordinates of each start and stop event in the IMD (see Figure 4.10). The table contents are listed in ascending temporal order (i.e. start or stop events for actors along with their position and size in the IMD). The execution table is filled with the appropriate data resulting from the sorted list of objects, and sorted again depending on the time that each event occurs (two events, start/stop for each object). It is feasible to have the execution table in text file by pressing the save button when the execution table window is active.

sec	Object	Action	Co-ordinates (Pos/Size)
0	Starting Logo	Start	6.0 , 2.5 / 8.0 , 8.0
0	Start Sound	Start	-1.0 ,-1.0 / -1.0 ,-1.0
4	Agora	Start	16.0 ,10.0 / 4.0 , 3.0
4	Zeus temple	Start	0.0 ,10.0 / 4.0 , 3.0
4	Stadium	Start	16.0 , 0.0 / 4.0 , 3.0
4	Start of Tour	Start	-1.0 ,-1.0 / -1.0 ,-1.0
4	Parthenon	Start	0.0 , 0.0 / 4.0 , 3.0
4	Athens (View)	Start	0.0 , 0.0 / 20.0 ,13.0
4	Starting Logo	Stop	
4	Start Sound	Stop	
14	Start of Tour	Stop	
14	Athens (View)	Stop	
15	Tour Video	Start	4.0 , 3.0 / 12.0 , 7.0
17	Historical facts	Start	4.0 , 0.0 / 12.0 , 3.0
25	Places to see	Start	0.0 , 3.0 / 4.0 , 7.0
37	Hotels	Start	16.0 ,13.0 / 4.0 , 7.0
41	Night life	Start	4.0 ,10.0 / 12.0 , 3.0
45	Tour Video	Pause	
45	Agora	Stop	
45	Zeus temple	Stop	
45	Stadium	Stop	
45	Parthenon	Stop	
47	End Logo	Start	4.0 , 3.0 / 12.0 , 7.0
47	End Sound	Start	-1.0 ,-1.0 / -1.0 ,-1.0
47	Places to see	Stop	
49	Historical facts	Stop	
53	Night life	Stop	
53	Hotels	Stop	

Figure 4.10. The IMD execution table, presentation actions in temporal ascending order including spatial information (position and size)

The IMD becomes persistent by saving it to a file. The file is in binary format and can be interpreted only by the tool. Another type of output is the "script". This is adopted for compatibility between authoring tools. The script, however, contains the declarative script representing the spatiotemporal relationships among the participating actors as the user has defined them.

4.3   Conclusions

In this chapter we presented an implemented authoring & verification methodology for IMD documents development. The IMD design is based on a theoretical model for spatiotemporal compositions in the context of multimedia presentations [Vaz98]. The tool may be used both for *prototyping* and *verification* of multimedia presentations or spatiotemporal compositions in general. As for the authoring phase, emphasis was put on the flexible definition of spatial and temporal relationships of the participating entities. The authoring phase consists mainly of declarative specifications of the spatial and temporal ordering of participating multimedia objects based on their spatial and temporal relationships.

The *verification* procedures give multiple tools to designers, preview their applications, in various ways: *spatial layouts* of the application window, *temporal layout* of parts (or the whole application), indicating the temporal duration and relationships among the participating objects and *animation (rendering)* of the application.

The *advantageous features* of the authoring tool are the following:

• Declarative & visual authoring methodology.

• Integrated Spatiotemporal IMD specification, taking into account the temporal and spatial features of the participating objects along with their spatiotemporal relationships. The methodology is based on a sound theoretical framework [Vaz98].

• Relative actor positioning in spatial and temporal domains. Moreover the object under concern may be related to different objects (i.e. "Object A to appear 10cm to the right of the bottom right corner of object B and 4 cm above the upper-left corner of object C" or "Object A to start 10sec after object B and 4 sec before object C")

As for *verification*, we provide a set of tools that enable the authors verify multiple aspects of their scenario and answer queries related to the spatiotemporal configuration of the IMD. The tools include screen layouts, temporal layouts and IMD animation tools.

The most important advantage of our design is that the authoring and the verification process are well integrated and interleaved so as the author is able to verify the authoring specification within the authoring procedure and environment.

The tool presented above may be extended towards interactive scenario integrity checking. The scenario integrity issue is crucial when designing a complex interactive scenario. The multitude of events and the related interactions that may occur in an IMD session may create a lot of potential evolution paths which are difficult to follow at authoring time, considering all potential implications.

5. Transformation of Declarative Specifications to Algorithmic Representation

The declarative representation, result of the authoring process described in the previous section, is close to human understanding. In order that this representation becomes usable (i.e. the scenario to be executed and the desired presentations take place), we need to transform it into a form closer to the machine so that it may be executed in an algorithmic context. In the case of pre-orchestrated scenarios, this is rather simple. The IMDs are not within this case, though. Most of the presentation actions are dependent on user actions or events that occur within the application (intra-IMD interaction). That would be the case of an interactive movie, for example, where the user and/or the actors' behavior would change the flow of the movie.

In this section we describe a scheme transforming IMD declarative representation into a set of algorithms that are "assembled" into a generic IMD template to form the specific application module. The process is illustrated in Figure 5.1.

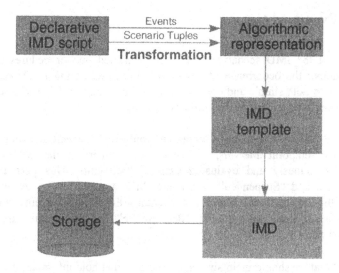

Figure 5.1. The transformation of the declarative IMD script into algorithmic executable form.

The declarative IMD script as a result from the authoring process, is translated into a set of procedures corresponding to the constituents of the scenario, namely: the events and the scenario tuples (including the synchronized presentation actions). The result of this process is a set of procedures specific to the IMD under concern. This set of procedures is integrated in a predefined IMD template, and the result is the specific algorithmic form of the IMD document. The IMD Template is a generic IMD execution module skeleton that includes several modules:

- IMD Initialization

- Scenario tuple manipulation (starting and stopping scenario tuples)

- Error Logging (storage of exceptions occurring at runtime),

- Presentation Engine: in charge of the multimedia objects presentation (starting, stopping, pausing and resuming temporal objects, or enabling and disabling buttons or displaying and hiding images).

- Events Detection & Evaluation mechanism (presented in further sections) along with generic algorithms for detection of all the Event types.

In the following subsections, we present the transformation of events and scenario tuples into algorithms.

5.1   Events

The events of the IMD scenario need to be translated into procedures that, when executed, detect the occurrence of such event instances during IMD session. This should apply to both simple and complex events. The transformation will be based on the event types as described in the previous sections.

Since we are dealing with a single thread environment, the event detection is carried out at regular temporal intervals, i.e. the events occurring in the IMD session are collected continuously and evaluated each T time units. This period of event collection is called "Suspended". When the IMD stops collecting events, it starts processing the collected information (i.e. evaluates the collected events) and triggers the appropriate actions. This period is called "Active". The system states are presented in detail in further sections.

It is evident that we should maintain some structures that hold information collected in "Suspended" periods and are exploited during "Active" ones. Hereby we refer to some of them that are needed in the algorithms mentioned later:

RecentEventsList: this list stores all the events raised during the last "Suspended" period state as well as during the consecutive "Active" one. During the "Active" period, only events related to media states are detected. When the system falls again in

"Suspended" state, the list RecentEventsList is initialized in order to collect the new raised events.

Update: this variable indicates whether the IMD Engine has triggered any presentation action during the last "Active" period. If any such action was triggered, then the execution of the module is repeated. This is due to the fact that the triggered action may raise some event that has to be detected.

HistoryList: this list stores all the simple events that have occurred since the start of the current IMD session. Moreover, for each event the corresponding temporal signature (according to the *Application Timer* indication) is also stored. This list is mainly used to provide information about the past of the application.

EventsList: this list includes all the events defined in the current scenario along with their member values, as they are defined in previous sections.

Hereafter, we refer to algorithms that are generated and later exploited by the Event Detection & Evaluation mechanism.

5.1.1   User Events

As already mentioned, these events are produced by input devices due to user actions (i.e. mouse or keyboard actions). These events are "Self-raised", i.e. they inform the system of their occurrence. When such an event is detected, the corresponding procedure (one for each type of event, e.g. mouse right click) takes charge of the event handling. The generic algorithm is the following:

```
If (event is in EventsList) then
        Update RecentEventsList
        Update HistoryList ( insert event
               attach Time indication )
```

Thus, for each such event in the IMD specification a corresponding procedure is produced.

5.1.2   Intra-objects Events

As already mentioned, these are the events that are generated by objects participating in the application. An intra-object event can be either *state-change* or *state*.

State-change events are generated by changes in the state of their *subject*. We distinguish the following cases:

- *Timer-indication event*: handled as described later for application and system events.

- *Button (object) click*: detected and handled in the same way as user events. The only difference is that in this case the appropriate algorithm is added for each button-object whose clicking is related to a defined event.

- *Temporal objects' state change events:* here we are interested in events related to the temporal state of an object (idle, active, and suspended) and the transition among these states. Most of these events are rather "detected" than "Self-raised", since the application itself is responsible for their generation. The only exception is the event raised when actor stops playing due to natural termination. When such an object state change action occurs, it is immediately followed by the two steps described below :

  ```
  Update RecentEventsList
  Update HistoryList ( insert event attach Time indication )
  ```

State events are not actual events and, therefore, not specifically detected by the application. A history of these events is not really needed since it cannot be referred to in any part of the scenario.

5.1.3   Application and System Events

These events are again "detected". In this case we are interested in all *application*, *system* and *timer-indication events*. The detection is handled by the *SpecialEvent()* procedure. If one of these events is defined in the scenario, it is detected by the appropriate procedure call, which takes place each T time units (the duration of the "Suspended" state period) and before any other action is triggered. Thus, the corresponding events are detected and the appropriate data structures are updated. The algorithm follows:

```
Procedure SpecialEvent(event)
       if type of event_expression is SystemSettings(DATE(instance)) then
       if (SystemDate= instance) then
              return true
       else
              return false
       else    // the event is a system time or ApplicationTimer or timer-indication event
       if (event_expression = TRUE) then
              Update RecentEventsList
              Update HistoryList (        insert event
                                          attach Time indication )
       End Procedure SpecialEvent(event)
```

For each such event a corresponding procedure is produced.

5.1.4   Synch Events

The synch events are "raised events", in the sense that they are created by the scenario tuples when they are starting or stopping their execution. Actually, they are raised by the procedures that enable and disable scenario tuples. More specifically, after a scenario tuple has been enabled/disabled by the corresponding procedure, the following algorithm is executed:

```
if (scenario tuple start/stop synch event has been defined) then
        Update RecentEventsList
        Update HistoryList (insert event attach Time indication)
```

5.1.5   Non-state Events

This category includes all the simple events, except the state and the synch ones. Each one of these events is related to a subject and an action as presented below:

```
Event E1
        Subject = Object1
        Action = Action1
```

The evaluating of non-state events is carried out by creating a procedure for each such event that has been defined in the scenario. These procedures have the same name as the corresponding events, and use the information kept in *RecentEventsList* in order to verify that the corresponding event has been raised in the current IMD session. They return *true* if the event has been raised; otherwise, they return *false*. For example, the following procedure is used for the evaluation of the simple non-state event E1:

```
Procedure E1( )
        If (event E1 is in RecentEventsList) then
                return true
        else
                return false
End of procedure E1()
```

The only case in which the procedure that handles the evaluation of a non-state event does not have the above structure, is in the case that it involves a SystemSettings(DATE()) event.

5.1.6   State Events

The state events are generated when an object falls into a desired temporal state (i.e. a video falls from the idle to the active state). A *state* event E2 is defined as follows:

```
Event E2
        Subject = Object2
        Action = <DesiredState>
```

The <DesiredState> refers to a set of possible states for Object2 and depends on the nature of the actor. For example, the states for a sound object care: active, idle, suspended.

As in the case of non-state events, evaluating state events implies the creation (during scenario transformation) of a procedure for each state event defined in the scenario. These procedures have the same name as the corresponding events. The difference is that state event evaluation procedures indicate whether the event is raised by checking the state of the object defined as *subject* of the event. As an example, the following procedure evaluates event E2 and returns true if the subject of the event is in DesiredState:

```
Procedure E2( )
        If (state of actor Object2 = DesiredState) then
                return true
        else
                return false
End of procedure E2( )
```

5.1.7   Complex Events

As mentioned earlier, such events are "detected" and if raised, they are not included in *HistoryList*. These events are evaluated by appropriate procedures that make use of the lists *HistoryList* and *RecentEventsList*. Event evaluation refers to the evaluation of the occurrence of an event or the satisfaction of a condition.

Hereafter we deal with the transformation of complex events included in the *start-* or *stop-* event expressions of scenario tuples. The evaluation of such events involves the transformation of complex events into procedural algorithms. The generic steps followed for the transformation are:

1. Evaluate all simple events appearing in the expression

2. Evaluate all complex events defined by functions in the expression

3. Apply all operators to the results of steps 1 and 2.

We have developed algorithms that correspond to the following algebraic composition functions, corresponding to the composition operators defined in previous chapters:

- $e := IN(e_1, t\_int)$: event e occurs when event e_1 occurs during the temporal interval t_int. The related algorithm follows:

```
//Detection of event "in specified temporal interval"
Procedure in(Event event ,Time Min, Time Max)
        if (Min is SystemTime instance) then
                if (Min <= current SystemTime <= Max) then
                        return true
        else if (Min is ApplicationTime instance) then
                if (Min <= Time Variable <= Max) then
                        return true
        else if (Min is System date) then
                if (Min <= current SystemDate <= Max) then
                        return true
        else
                return false
End Procedure in(event , Time Min , Time Max)
```

- $e := ANY(k, e_1, ..., e_n)$: This event occurs when at least any k of the events $e_1, ..., e_n$ occur since the IMD start. The sequence of occurrence is irrelevant.

```
// detection of "any k" of the events included in ListofEvents
Procedure any(integer k, ListofEvents ev_list)
    if (none of the events in ev_list appears in RecentEventsList) then
        return false
    else
        integer number_found = 0
        for each event in ev_list
            if (event is in RecentEventsList) or (event is in HistoryList) then
                number_found = number_found + 1
            if number_found = k then
                return true
            if number_found < k then
                return false
End of procedure any(k, ev_list)
```

- e :== after(e_1,t,e_2), event e occurs when e_1,e_2 both occurred and the temporal signature of e_1 is t time units smaller than the corresponding signature of e_2. If t is null then the procedure detects simply the sequence of events

```
// detection of events "B following A after t time units"
Procedure interval (Event A, Temp_interval t, Event B)
    if (t >= 0) then
        Event e1 = A
        Event e2 = B
    else
        Event e1 = B
        Event e2 = A
    if (e2 is not in RecentEventsList) then
        return false
    if (t = 0) then
        if e1 is in RecentEventsList then
                return true
    else
        return false
    if (e1 is not in RecentEventsList) and (e1 is not in EventsList) then
        return false
    if ( (ApplicationTime - |t|) = e1.last_occurrence.time_stamp) then
        return true
    else
        return false
End Procedure interval (A, t, B)
```

- e = SEQ(e_1,...,e_n): This event occurs when all events e_1,...,e_n occur in the order appearing in the list.

```
// detection of a "sequence of events" as listed in Ev_List
Procedure seq(ListofEvents ev_list)
if (last of ev_List is not in RecentEventsList) then
        return false
else
        Event current_event = get first of ev_List
        if (current_event is not in HistoryList) then
                return false
        else
                low_limit = n-th (last) occurrence of
                        current_event in the HistoryList
                push low_limit into timestack
                while (ev_List is not empty)
                        current_event = first of ev_List
```

```
                    next_time = time of n-th (last)
                    occurrence of current_event in HistoryList
                    if (next_time < first item of timestack) then
                    // order of events is broken
                            return false
                    else
                    // search for previous occurrences of curr. ev.
                            found = false
                            j = 1 //last occurrence of the oldest event
                            while (found is false)
                                    prev_oc=(n-j)th occur of curr_ev in HistList
                                    if (prev_oc < low_limit) then
                                            found = true
                                    if (pr_oc >= first item in timestack) then
                                            j = j + 1 //continue going back
                                    if (pr_oc < first item in timestack) then
                                            return false
                            end while
                            push next_time into timestack
            end while
            return true
    End Procedure seq(Ev_List)
```

- $e = ANYNEW(k,e_1,...,e_n)$: This event occurs when at least any k of the events $e_1,...,e_n$ occurred in period corresponding to the most recent "Suspended" state (i.e. the last time that the system searched for these events). The sequence of occurrence is irrelevant. For example, in an interactive game a user proceeds to the next level when he is successful in two out of three tests that generate the corresponding events e_1, e_2, and e_3.

```
    // detection of "any new k" of events included in ev_List,
    Procedure anynew(integer k, ListofEvents ev_List)
            integer number_found = 0
            for each event in ev_List
                    if (event is in RecentEventsList) then
                            number_found = number_found + 1
                    if (number_found = k) then
                            return true
                    if (number_found < k) then
                            return false
    End of procedure anynew(k, ListofEvents)
```

5.2   Scenario Tuples

A scenario tuple has to be transformed into a set of algorithms, each one corresponding to each of its parts: Start_event, Stop_event, Action_list and Synch Events. In this section we discuss all but the Action_List transformation. The Presentation engine that interprets the temporal operations and triggers the appropriate presentation actions, at runtime, handles this issue, which is presented in further sections.

5.2.1   Start Stop Event Detection Handlers

For each tuple we need handlers for detecting the start event and the stop event. Each of these handlers is a procedure that returns "true", if the event is raised, and "false", otherwise. Assume a tuple T1 and its start event *e1* which may be arbitrarily complex. The start event of the tuple is detected by the handler T1started as follows:

```
Procedure T1_started()
if e1 is true
        return true
else
        return false
end procedure T1_started()
```

The procedure corresponding to "Stop_event" (T1stopped) is produced in a similar way.

It is clear that for each scenario tuple in an IMD, the corresponding procedures for the start/stop events are generated. In Table 5.1 we present the mapping conventions for translation of the declarative start/stop event into the corresponding procedure. The translation is carried out according to the following rules:

Declarative IMD script		Procedural representation
"("	->	"("
")"	->	")"
"|"	->	"OR "
","	->	"AND"
"NOT"	->	"NOT
Simple event "event1"	->	"event1"
"A:t:B"	->	" interval(A,t,B)"
"IN(event,min,max)"	->	"in (event,min,max)"
"ANY(k;e_1;e_2;...;e_n)"	->	"any(k, nlist)" where nlist is the list (e_1,e_2,...,e_n)
"ANYNEW(k;e_1;e2;...;e_n)"	->	"anynew(k, nlist)" where nlist is the list (e_1,e2,...,e_n)
"SEQ(e_1;e2;...;e_n)"	->	"seq(nlist)" where nlist is the list (e_1,e2,...,e_n)
"StartApp"	->	"ApplicationTime= 0"

Table 5.1. Event composition operator and function transformation rules

For instance, assuming a scenario tuple T1 with the start event: "e1:3:e2 \| ANY(2;e1;e4;e3) ; NOT (e5) " where e1,...,e5 are simple events defined in an IMD, then the procedure T1started() is as follows :

```
Procedure T1started()
System TIME // TIME represents the global clock of the IMD
  if (interval(e1,3, e2) OR any(2,e1,e4,e3) AND
    NOT ( e5 ) is true) then
        return true
  else
        return false
end procedure T1started()
```

5.2.2   Enabling and Disabling Scenario Tuples

The next step would be to create handlers for enabling/disabling scenario tuples. For each scenario tuple T1 the corresponding enabling (T1Enable) and disabling (T1Disable) handlers are created. We also need to know if it is already enabled or disabled, since we may not trigger an action that would bring the tuple into a state it is already in. Assume a scenario tuple T1. The following algorithms trigger the execution of this tuple and, when the Stop_event is raised, they stop it and the actors enabled by this. The corresponding algorithms follows:

```
//Enabling the tuple
Procedure T1Enable()
  if ((T1. Start_event = true) and (T1 is disabled) and
    ((T1 is not in ActiveTuples list) then
          enable T1
end Procedure T1enable()

//Disabling the tuple
Procedure T1disable()
  if ((T1.Stop_event = true) and (T1 is enabled) and (T1 is not
    in Active tuples) list) then
          stop all actors enabled by T1
          disable T1
end Procedure T1disable()
```

We also consider the case in which the start and stop events are raised simultaneously. In such case, the tuple should not alter its state. The following procedure is applied:

```
Procedure T1simultaneous_start_stop_events()
  if (simultaneous(T1.Start_event, T1.Stop_event) = true) then
      do not alter the state of tuple T1
```

The term "simultaneously" in this case should be interpreted as "the two events occurred in the same 'Suspended' system period".

6. Rendering Interactive Multimedia Scenarios

The IMD scenario model described so far is primarily related to the definition of a scenario and its components. Once we have the IMD we are concerned about ways to present, deliver it to the target audience. In order to present (we will further use the term *render*) the media objects according to the scenario tuples (i.e. starting and stopping synchronized presentation of media objects), we must create a rendering scheme capable of playing a scenario in such a way that all properties of the model are satisfied. Rendering is the process of enforcing the presentation specifications of the IMD scenario, i.e. when, where, for how long and under what transformations each media object will be presented. Thus, it is essential to state the requirements of such a rendering scheme before continuing with its design. A rendering scheme should be able to do the following:

- Detect events generated by the system, the user or the actors

- Evaluate these events against the start/stop event expressions of each scenario tuple

- Activate the appropriate tuples asynchronously

- Perform synchronized presentation actions according to the scenario tuples' specifications.

- Handle exceptions

- Maintain the Quality of Service (QoS)

In the following we present two implemented designs we have carried out in this topic. A single threaded generic one and a multithreaded appropriate for the latest technological demands arising from the WWW.

6.1   A Single Threaded Approach

In previous chapters we have presented the transformation of the declarative IMD script into algorithmic form. Once the IMD scenario has been transformed into algorithmic form, we need to specify an execution plan. In other words, to define the scenario rendering strategy. This task is rather straightforward in "pre-orchestrated" applications while in the case of IMDs with rich interaction, it becomes more complicated. Indeed, interaction makes difficult to know in advance the spatial and temporal presentation features of the participating objects.

The objective here is the elaboration of a mechanism for IMD scenario rendering. It is evident that executing complex IMDs may be a complicated task, taking into account the large set of possible events that may occur in the application context, the number of actors participating in the application, as well as the various potential combinations of these parameters.

The IMD template (see chapter five) includes modules for manipulating the IMD session features as described in the previous section. The IMD specific values for those features are plugged into the IMD template and a self-standing IMD instance is formed. The execution of this application carries out the rendering of the scenario, exploiting the occurring events, the history of the IMD and the actor states.

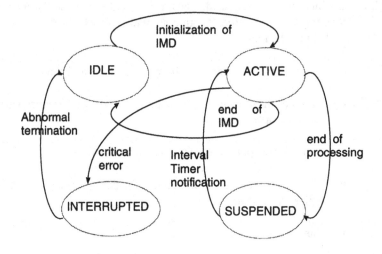

Figure 6.1. State diagram of the Multimedia Scenario Rendering Engine (MSRE) .

The life-cycle of an IMD instance session, includes the following phases:

- Initialization of the system that executes the scenario

- Detection evaluation of the events occurring in the IMD context

- Processing of the information related to the IMD functional entities (such as events, media states, etc.),

- Triggering of the presentation actions

- Exception handling

- Termination of the application.

These procedures are carried out while the IMD session is in different states. The system's behavior is illustrated in the state-transition diagram in Figure 6.1. Initially, the system is "Idle", waiting for a message to start the execution of the scenario. When such a message is received, the system passes through an initialization phase and falls into the "Active" state. In this state it processes the information available and triggers the execution of the corresponding actions. The MSRE (see Figure 6.3) manipulates the following pieces of information:

- The currently raised events. Just after the IMD session only the event "StartOfApplication" is raised.

- The history of the events storing all the events that have occurred since the session start (initially no events exist in that table).

- The states of the actors participating in the application.

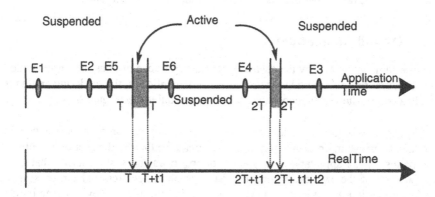

Figure 6.2. The states of the system during an IMD session

When the processing of the available information is complete the system falls into the "Suspended" state while the "Interval Timer" is started again. In this state the system does not trigger any presentation actions, but it collects all events appearing in the context of the application. The Interval Timer expires after T time units (sufficient for collecting the events that occurred as well as for making the system react to these events) and generates a notification message ("Interval Timer Notification message") that indicates the end of the events' collection phase ("Suspended" state). Upon reception of this message the IMD falls again into the "Active" state, in order to process the events collected during the "Suspended" temporal interval and to trigger the corresponding presentation actions. When the information processing is complete the system becomes "Suspended" again to collect more events. The aforementioned procedure is repeated until the event "EndOfApplication", that indicates the end of the scenario, is raised.

The Application Timer plays an important role in the MSRE architecture, indicating the "Application Time" (amount of time units elapsed since the start of the application). The global clock is incremented by T time units each time the system becomes "Active". Figure 6.2 illustrates the whole procedure in the temporal domain. Assume E2, E3, E4, E5, E6 are events defined in the scenario, the temporal intervals indicated as shadowed parts in the time axis are the intervals during which the system is "Active" and t1, t2 correspond to their arbitrary duration. At this point a problem may arise since the Application Time and the System Real Time indication may differ significantly at the end of a long IMD. During the scenario execution various exceptions may raise. This issue is further presented in the Scenario Rendering section.

When an exception is raised the MSRE evaluates whether it is a critical one or not. If the exception is not critical the system will try to bring itself to a desirable state; the system handles the exception and terminates the application normally. At this point the system falls into the "Idle" state. If the exception is critical, then the special event "CriticalError" is raised and the system falls into the "Interrupted" state.

6.1.1   Overall Architecture

The algorithms generated by the scenario translating procedure must be implemented in a procedural programming language. As already mentioned, the rendering engine is actually a composite system consisting of various modules (see Figure 6.3).

The "Application Engine" module corresponds to the application running instance. In this context various interactions may occur (originated either by the user or by entities participating in the application, or events coming from the system itself) that may alter the flow of the application under certain circumstances (critical errors, system timer's notification message, messages coming from resources or devices used by the application, etc.). The Application module is the main *event* generator that "feeds" the execution mechanism with all events occurring in the application.

The "Event Detection & Evaluation" module receives the events produced by the application and subsequently filters and evaluates them. The events may be atomic or complex according to the authoring specifications. The detection and evaluation mechanism is based on the recently raised events, the application's event history and the states of the media participating in the application. The output of the "Event Detection & Evaluation" module is a set of events that were detected and that are included in the IMD scenario. This set ("Raised Events") is the input to the Application engine. The mechanism is described in more details in the sub-section that follows.

The Application Engine module is invoked each time the Interval timer expires and sends a notification message. This module actually executes the scenario and is responsible for starting and stopping the scenario tuples, as well as for the execution of the actions appearing in scenario tuples' action list. This implies the synchronized execution of the media presentation actions as defined in the scenario tuples. Actually the Application Engine, having processed the, potentially complex, presentation expressions in the scenario tuples (i.e. synchronized presentation of several media objects), produces low-level commands for presentation of media objects. Moreover, runtime errors may occur in the application. These errors do not terminate the flow of the application unless they are critical. All errors are reported in the *Runtime Errors* log file.

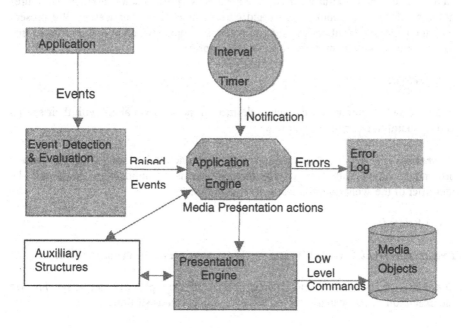

Figure 6.3. The architecture of the MSRE system

The *Presentation Engine* module is responsible for single media object presentations.

The MSRE architecture presented here is generic and may be implemented on any single thread platform. Subsequently, the procedures of events processing and media presentation cannot be concurrent. The *Interval Timer* serves the purpose of triggering the execution of presentation actions after a period of length T time units, during which the events processing takes place. The *Interval Timer* starts the temporal interval T and notifies accordingly so that the systems falls into the *Active* state (processing the information available and triggering presentation actions), or to the *Suspended* state (collecting the events which occur in the application).

In the following sub-section we discuss the auxiliary structures that are maintained so that the above-described way of handling an Interactive Multimedia presentation is feasible.

6.1.2   Auxiliary Structures

It is evident that the application flow depends on information we maintain about the present and the past states of the application. The information we need is related to: the set of the active actors, the history of events, the set of the enabled scenario tuples, etc. In order to manipulate this multitude of information we need to maintain a set of data structures and auxiliary variables. Hereafter we present some auxiliary structures holding information about the past and current state of the application. We present only the most important ones to support reader's comprehension of the algorithms that follow. We classify them in the following categories:

Actor related:

Actors: a list containing all the actors defined in the scenario along with their spatial and temporal transformation attributes.

ActorsEnabled: this list stores the currently active actors (i.e. media objects that are presented), along with the starting time (in terms of application time) and the identifier of the scenario tuple that activated the actor.

Event Related:

Events, HistoryList, RecentEventsList: These were presented in chapter five.

SynchEvents: the synch events defined in the scenario tuples in order to synchronize the execution of the scenario tuples, as defined in previous sections.

Scenario Tuple related:

ScenarioTuples: the scenario tuples defined in the current scenario along with their attributes' member values as they are defined in previous sections.

ActiveTuples: This list stores the identifiers of the scenario tuples that were triggered at previous executions of the Application Engine and need to be ignored at the following ones.

TuplesWithActivity: This list stores the identifiers of the scenario tuples that were triggered (i.e. their Start_event was triggered) during the current execution of the Application Engine. Each time that the system becomes Suspended, this list is concatenated with the ActiveTuples List.

TuplesEnabled: this list stores the identifiers of the tuples that are currently enabled (i.e. the actions in the action list are currently being executed and have not finished yet). Also the starting time (in terms of application time) of the tuple as well as the number of the pending instruction streams are stored.

Application related:

Time: this variable simulates the global IMD clock and indicates the time that has elapsed since the IMD start. The value of the Variable is increased by T time units each time the system becomes suspended.

Update : it was also presented in chapter five, and indicates whether the IMD Engine has triggered any presentation action during the last "Active" period. If any such action was triggered, then the execution of the module is repeated. This is due to the fact that the triggered action may raise some event that has to be detected.

6.1.3   Event Detection and Evaluation

The generic *Event Detection & Evaluation* module that is provided by the IMD Template (depicted in Figure 6.4), handles the detection of events. This mechanism exploits the event detection procedures generated during the scenario translation procedure, and the event instances occurring in an IMD execution session. *The Event Detection & Evaluation* module is executed at appropriate temporal intervals, i.e. each T Application time units, when the system becomes Active.

The events are produced by the entities involved in the IMD session, such as: the system, the user, the scenario tuples, the actors, the related timers, and may be classified in the IMD context into:

- *Self-raised,* events that inform the detection mechanism about their occurrence through the operating system. Such events are the input events, i.e. the event mouse click is triggered by system monitors.

- *Detected,* events that are raised when some process evaluates a condition as true. Such events are the complex and the state-change ones. In this case a mechanism has to evaluate a condition that evaluates the event's occurrence.

The events occurred during an IMD session are directed to an initial *Event Filter* mechanism. This mechanism selects only those events that are included in the *Events List* and, thus, are of interest to the IMD. The output of this procedure is a list of *Self-Raised Events*. Then the IMD related structures (RecentEventsList, HistoryList etc.) are updated and the evaluation phase starts. The result of this procedure is a new set of *Detected Events*. These events together with the *Self-raised Events* are the new *Raised Events*. These events are sent into the Application Engine that triggers the appropriate presentation actions.

We further describe the event detection mechanism. At first place each time the Interval timer expires, the *RecentEventsList* is checked and the simple events from the IMD scenario that are found the list are raised using the corresponding procedures. Thus the raised events are produced. All the simple events that have been defined in the scenario (including synch events) are inserted into the *HistoryList*. During application execution, this list will be updated with all the occurrences (attached with their temporal signature) of the application's simple events. What is important is that *HistoryList* holds information only for the events that have explicitly been defined during the authoring process. Therefore, the only events handled (detected and evaluated) by the event detection mechanism during the application are the ones predefined as events of interest.

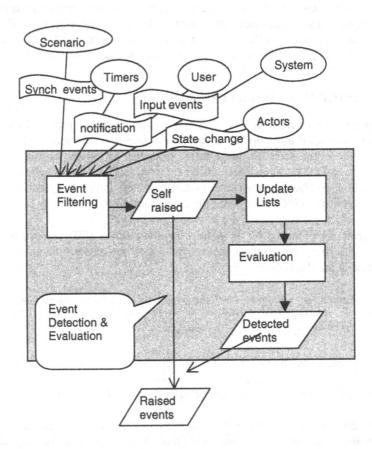

Figure 6.4. The Event Detection Mechanism (activated on Timer Notification Messages)

The detection of events potentially updates the related data structures in order to inform the system that a specific event has been raised. We handle each event according to the category of the entity it is related to.

The evaluation of complex event is based on information stored in the auxiliary structures about the past and current state of the IMD, and evaluates each event procedure (as resulted in the transformation procedures) according to that information. For each event type there is a predefined procedure (as presented in chapter five) that evaluates such events. So for each such event in the IMD scenario there is a corresponding procedure generated according to its type. During an IMD session there are occurrences (i.e. creations of new instances of events) which are detected by invoking the aforementioned procedures. The evaluation algorithm is as follows:

```
Procedure Event_Evaluation()
for each event in EventsList
        if event = true // the corresponding procedure is called
                update Recent EventsList
                update HistoryList
```

6.1.4   Scenario Rendering Algorithms

In this subsection we present the algorithms that are in charge of rendering the scenario and that correspond to the modules appearing in Figure 6.4.

The main body of the execution algorithm is generic, so it is the same for all the IMDs. Hereafter, we present the initialization procedure that is invoked when the execution of the scenario starts. This procedure initializes the auxiliary structures and the application log file. It also starts the Application Timer and the Interval Timer for the first time.

```
Initialization Procedure
        Insert all actors defined in scenario into the Actors list.
        Insert all events defined in scenario into the Events list.
        Insert all sc. tuples defined in scenario into Tuples list.
        Insert all Syn.Ev defined in sc. tup into SynchEvents.
        Initialize the media participating in the application.
        Initialize all the auxiliary data structures and variables
        Create a new empty Error log file.
        Initialize the Application Timer (Time =0).
        Start the Interval Timer (expires after T time units).
```

As mentioned before each time that the Interval Timer the system evaluates the events that have occurred and trigger presentation actions. In the sequel we present the algorithm that is activated each time that the *Interval Timer* expires. Then a notification message is raised and the Timer Notification procedure is executed. This procedure initializes again the *Active Tuples* and *TuplesWithActivity* lists so as to detect which scenario tuples should be activated and it activates them (through the *Playscenario* procedure) in this repetition list. Since the presentation actions that are triggered by the *Playscenario* procedure may create events that in turn may activate other scenario tuples, we have to repeat them until no further event is created. The repetition is handled by the *Update* variable.

Timer Notification Procedure
If (notification message is sent by the Interval timer) then
        Set ActiveTuples list to null
        Set Update variable to true.
        while Update variable is true
                Set Update variable to false.
                Set TuplesWithActivity list to null.
                call PlayScenario procedure
                Concatenate ActiveTuples and TuplesWithActivity.
        end while
        Restart the Interval Timer
        Increment the Time variable by T.
        Set RecentEvents list to null

The procedure PlayScenario is the core of IMD execution mechanism and is generated after translating the Scenario Tuples defined in the scenario, which will be described hereafter. This procedure:

- evaluates Application Timer, System and timer events, and updates the RecentEvents List,

- detects all scenario Start/Stop events and changes the state of the corresponding tuples accordingly

- triggers the appropriate synchronized presentation actions processing according to the instruction streams of all enabled tuples.

The procedure is as follows:

PlayScenario Procedure
        detect application_timer event & update HistoryList
        detect events with timer as subject & update HistoryList
        detect all system (date or time) events & update HistoryList
        for each tuple in ScenarioTuples
                if   (start and stop events of tuple are raised simultaneously) then
                     put scenario tuple in Active tuples list
                if   (start event of scenario tuple is raised) and
                     (scenario tuple is disabled) and
                     (scenario tuple in not in ActiveTuples) then
                        Update = true
                        enable tuple
                        set tuple's start synch event = true
                        update HistoryList
                if   (tuple. Stop_event is true) and
                     (tuple is enabled) and
                     (tuple is not in Active tuples list) then
                        Update = true
                        stop all actors enabled by tuples
                        disable tuple
                        set the tuple.Stop_synch event = true
                        update HistoryList
        for each tuple in ActiveTuples

```
for each instruction stream
    for each action
        if (tuple is not in TuplesWithActivity)
        then
                TuplesWithActivity = TuplesWithActivity + tuple
                Update = true
                apply the operator on the actor   // call to Presentation Engine
                Update ActorsEnabled              // add/ remove actor,
                                                  // depending on type of action
            if  (action is the last of the instruction stream) then
                disable the tuple
```

6.1.5   Presentation Engine

As it is clear from the previous algorithm, when a scenario tuple is enabled, all the instruction streams appearing in the action list are simultaneously triggered. The execution of all instructions streams appearing in a scenario tuple implies the extraction of appropriate algorithms for each case. We may encounter the following cases, based on the type of TAC operation that appears first in the instruction stream:

• If the TAC operator in the first action is >, || or |>, the execution algorithm is the following:

```
for action in instructions stream
if      (scenario tuple is enabled) and
        (related time offset + triggering time of instructions stream = Current Application
           Time ) and
    (scenario tuple is not in ActiveTuples list) then
                Apply operator to the actor
```

• If the instructions stream includes only one action, regardless of the operator applying on the media, the execution algorithm is the following simple one:

```
if (scenario tuple is enabled) and (scenario tuple in ActiveTuples list)
        Apply the operator to the actor
```

• If the operator on the first action is <, the first action is used as a condition that needs to be fulfilled in order to start executing the other actions of the instructions stream. The following execution algorithm is used:

```
if      (scenario tuple is enabled) and
        (state of actor in first action of the instructions stream is idle ) and
        (scenario tuple is not in ActiveTuples list) then
                enable the instructions stream
        for each action in instructions stream (except first one)
            if      (instructions stream is enabled) and
                    (related time offset + triggering time of instructions stream = Current
                    Application Time ) and
                    (scenario tuple is not in ActiveTuples list) then
                        Apply the operator to the actor
```

• If the operator "Λ" appears on the instructions stream, then no other operator is allowed to appear in this instructions stream. When a set of actors are related to the operator "Λ" they start their execution simultaneously, and when one of these actors stops, all the other actors stop their execution. The execution algorithm is the following one:

if   (scenario tuple is enabled)   and
      (scenario tuple is not in ActiveTuples list) then
              Start all actors appearing in instructions stream

if   (any actor in instructions stream becomes idle) then
              Stop all actors appearing in instructions stream

6.2   A Multithreaded Approach

The approach described above is generic but it has some important shortcoming due to the lack of parralelism in detection of events and execution of presentation actions:

• The events occurring during suspended state duration cannot be detected ans there fore they are lost

• The temproral interval that corresponds to the active period is not counted in the system timers. Therefore after many iterations the real time and the system time differ significantly resulting wrong overall synchronisation.

Thus there is motivation for an alternative rendring approach that will eliminate the above problems. Such a system is presented in this subsection. The implementation framework should support inherently the following features:

• Concurrent processes (i.e. a set of instruction streams running in parallel)

• Object creation and manipulation in order to be able to support explicitly the theoretical model presented before as it is clearly defined over a set of separate entities (i.e. scenarios, tuples, actors, events)

• Distribution features, as the objects may be located in any place (URL) on the Internet.

The system implementation is based on Java and other accompanying technologies due to its appealing features such as built- in multi-thread support, cross-platform compatibility. Moreover all WWW browsers support Java to a great extent thus making, the presentation of an IMD feasible in any WWW browser.

We implemented the system in a client-server approach. Both the client and the server, are implemented in Java and are, therefore, portable through a variety of platforms. The communication between them is performed exclusively using the RMI (Remote Method Invocation) protocol [J97a], a technology to seamlessly distribute Java objects (in our case IMDs and media objects) across the Internet and Intranets.

RMI allows Java objects to call methods of other Java objects. These methods can return primitive types and object references, but they can also return objects by-value, a feature unique to RMI among its related technologies (CORBA, DCOM). The continuous media, video and sound, are retrieved by the client from http servers specified in the scenario, and presented with the aid of Java Media Framework (JMF)[1] [J97b] which specifies an unified architecture, messaging protocol and programming interface for media rendering, media capture, and conferencing. JMF APIs support the synchronization, control, processing, and presentation of compressed streaming and stored time-based media, including video and audio. Streaming media is supported, where videos and sound are reproduced while they are being downloaded without being stored locally. This feature is extensively exploited in the system described here.

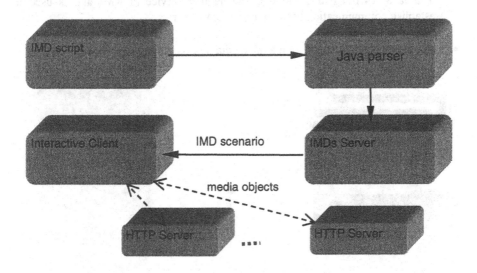

Figure 6.5. An IMD lifecycle

The lifecycle of an IMD in our system appears in Figure 6.5. The IMD script (actors, events, scenario tuples) produced by the authoring phase, is parsed and translated into corresponding Java objects that can be stored in the server using the Java Serialization services [J97a]. Finally the client may request a scenario from the server, retrieve and present it to the user by retrieving the media from the appropriate http servers.

---

[1] Currently, JMF is implemented only for Wintel platforms, thus the IMD client can only be executed in such platforms. It is expected that soon there will be implementation on other platforms.

6.2.1   The Server

The key elements of the system are the IMD objects, containing specifications for actors and the presentation scenario, and the handling of user and internal interactions. However, a scenario does not include the media objects data ,but only references to their locations in the form of URLs. The system architecture is illustrated in Figure 6.6. The server functionality is provided through the collaboration of three modules. These are:

- The actual Multimedia Document Server (MDS), responsible for the delivery of IMD objects to the client

- The Java RMI registry, which is the naming service of RMI and is used to establish communication between client and server

- The set of http servers on which the media objects resides.

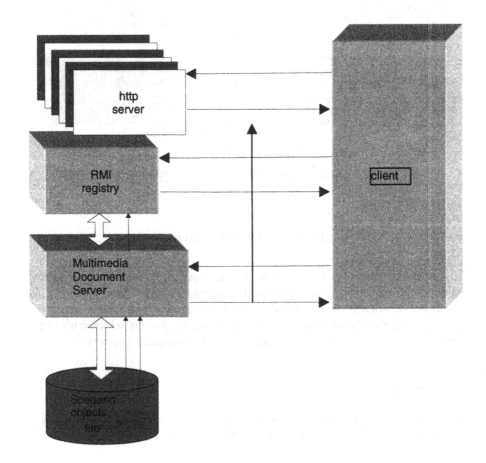

Figure 6.6. The server architecture and the communication with the client

The actions that take place during an IMD session are described hereafter. When the MDS is started, it scans a file that contains all IMD objects and stores their names and descriptions. Afterwards, it registers itself to the RMI registry and waits for client requests. When there is a client request for an IMD, the corresponding IMD object is accessed through the RMI registry, and through remote method invocation the IMD names, descriptions and scenarios are retrieved from the server. During the IMD session, whenever a media object (video, sound, image, text) is to be presented, the client communicates with the respective http server (through calls to the JMF in the case of video and sound) and presents the media object directly from the remote machine without storing it locally.

The separation of the scenarios from the media enhances the flexibility of the system, while giving greater control over a potential layer for QoS maintenance. The high availability of http servers can be used for massive distribution and replication of media; thereby reducing load on any individual server whereas one server may serve the requests for scenarios (time-independent and usually a few kilobytes in size).

6.2.2   Rendering Scheme Architecture - The Client

The task of the client is to present the IMD scenario according to the script specifications. In this subsection we present the client architecture. Our scheme mainly consists of two sets of modules. The first includes the modules aiming at presenting a scenario, while the second one is composed of the modules in charge of event detection and evaluation. These two sets work together in order to present a scenario to the end user. The basic idea behind this design is to use the first set to start a scenario, and then use the second one to control the flow of presentation for that scenario. We shall now elaborate on the architecture describing the implemented Java classes of our modules.

Each element of a scenario (i.e. tuples, events and actors) is represented as a different Java class. Therefore, we have a set of classes as follows:

- *ScenarioPlayer* class and a *TuplePlayer* class: are capable of handling an IMD scenario and a scenario tuple respectively

- *Actor* class: serves as the super-class of the classes that correspond to presentable media objects and user interface elements, namely: *Video, Image, Sound, Text, Button, Label* and *Timer*

- *AppEvent* class: stores information on all the events that may occur in the specific IMD session.

Apart from these we have also defined a few other classes that are essential to our scheme. The *InstructionStreamPlayer* class is responsible for synchronized presentation of media objects. We also have a set of listener classes that are in charge of presentation of a single media object and detect all events related to the single object presented. As an example, in order to show a video on the screen we should use an instance of the *VideoListener* class. Furthermore, that particular instance would have to be responsible for detecting all events associated with the video, such as the end of the video. Another fundamental class in our design is the *EventEvaluator* class, which is in charge of evaluating the start and stop events of all involved tuples each time a simple event occurs, and sends the appropriate messages to the *ScenarioPlayer*.

When an IMD scenario is to be presented, the following steps are executed. First, a *ScenarioPlayer* and an *EventEvaluator* object are created. The former generates a "StartApp" (start application) event. This is a special kind of event that denotes the start the IMD session and may appear in one or more tuples as their start event, meaning that the action part of the tuples will start playing as soon as the scenario starts. This event is sent to the *EventEvaluator* that determines which tuples are to be started and tells the *ScenarioPlayer* to start them. The *ScenarioPlayer* then creates the corresponding *TuplePlayer* objects. Each *TuplePlayer* creates as many *InstructionStreamPlayer* objects as necessary. The *InstructionStreamPlayer*s present media objects according to the scenario specifications by creating the appropriate listener objects. A listener object is created for each media object presented and each listener is paired with an instance of the *EvaluatorNotifier* class. This class's sole purpose is to furnish the listeners with a set of methods to send messages to the *EventEvaluator*. For example, when a *VideoListener* or a *SoundListener* detects the end of their corresponding media object they use the "sendStopEvent" method of the *EvaluatorNotifier* class to pass that message to the *EventEvaluator*. As the IMD session continues, more actors start and stop and events keep generating. *EventEvaluator* collects all these events and in collaboration with *ScenarioPlayer* defines the flow of the presentation. This is achieved by having the *ScenarioPlayer* start or stop the appropriate tuples, by creating new *TuplePlayer* objects or by destroying the ones that should stop. When a tuple must be interrupted, all the participating actors are interrupted (if they are active) and the appropriate synch event (if one exists for the tuple) is sent to the *EventEvaluator*. Finally, there comes a point that a tuple with action "ExitApplication" --another special action that denotes the end of a scenario-- starts and automatically all media stop playing and the scenario finishes. The procedure so far and the interdependencies among the instantiated classes are depicted in Figure 6.7.

One of our main concerns when designing this rendering scheme, was to be able to detect all events generated by the IMD sessions. We would also like to minimize the effect of an object failure in the IMD session (i.e. in the case the site holding the media data goes down) in order to avoid side effects to other actors so that scenario presentation would not crash. Therefore, we have implemented the *TuplePlayer*, *InstructionStreamPlayer*, listeners, *EvaluatorNotifier* and *EventEvaluator* classes as threads. The first three guarantees us that all actors are separate entities that do not affect one another; the two remaining classes make certain that we detect all events.

The rendering scheme includes two main tasks: detecting and evaluating all events, so as to start and interrupt scenario tuples on the basis of these events, and presenting media objects according to the specifications of the instruction streams in the scenario tuples. In the following subsections we present these tasks in detail.

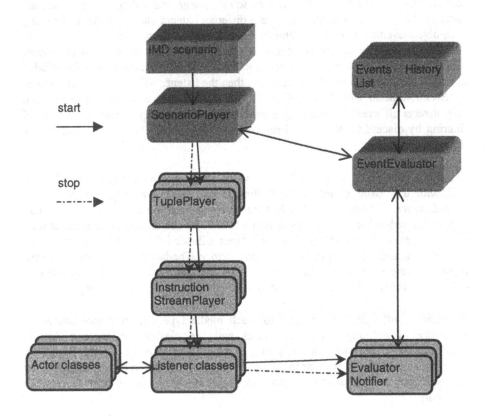

Figure 6.7. The architecture of the client for IDM scenario execution

6.2.3   Event Handling

Detecting Events

In the current client architecture, we deal with four categories of events: inter-object, intra-object, user and application events. At this point our rendering scheme is able to detect all kinds of events except inter-object events. The reason for this are the constraints imposed by the existing Java implementation; though, this may change in the future. Hereafter we shall examine the way our system handles each event category in detail.

Intra-object Events

This is the most significant category of events as it encompasses all events corresponding to media objects, such as sound, image and video. We have already stated that for each media type, there is a different listener class capable of detecting intra-object events related to the object. For example, a listener starts a video object,. The listener will handle that event and decide whether or not the event is significant for the scenario. If the event is of interest to the scenario (this means that it is included in one of the start/stop event expressions), then the listener will dispatch that event to the *EventEvaluator* with the use of the *EvaluatorNotifier*. In this stage the listener not only detects all events concerning a media object but also performs some kind of filtering by discarding all events irrelevant to the scenario. This is clarified by the following examples:

Assume a video named "v1". When the video starts execution (in section 3.2.5 we deal with this issue in more detail) then it will send a message to its' paired *VideoListener*. The listener will collect that event and ask the *ScenarioPlayer* if there is an event with subject = "v1" and action = "start". If such an event exists (i.e. it is an interesting event for the IMD), then the listener will send the event together with the actor that caused it ("v1") to the *EvaluatorNotifier*. The latter will in turn update the internal storage structures of our scheme (to be examined later) with the new state of video "v1" and then forward the event to the *EventEvaluator* for processing.

By using a different listener class for each media type, we guarantee maximum flexibility in defining detectable events and the classes are more viable to modifications due to Java as we only have to correct a small piece of code. By having a separate instance of the appropriate class for each media type, we minimize the consequences of a media-object problem that may occur (for instance a network problem).

User-Events

User events are either mouse events or keyboard events. As these events are not related to a specific media type, we adopt a different strategy for their evaluation. The key point with this kind of events is that there is no indication of when they will happen and that they cannot be assigned to any actor. For example a user event may be generated when the user presses key "F2" and this may occur many times during and IMD session. Thus, we must find a new way of capturing these events. The approach we adopted was to create a number of user-event listener objects directly from the start of the IMD sessions. For example, if the scenario author has defined three user-events: the pressing of key "F2", a mouse click and a mouse double-click then we shall create three listeners; one for "F2", one for the click and one for the double-click. These listeners are implemented as a part of the Java language. Their instantiation occurs right after we create the instance of the *ScenarioPlayer* class, which will hold the scenario to be presented. In this way we ensure that all user-events will be detected right from the start.

Once a user-event occurs, the action course is somewhat different to the one in the case of intra-object events. The event is not sent to an *EvaluatorNotifier*, as there is no need to check whether or not it is of interest to the scenario. We are certain it is of interest as we have only created listeners for events mentioned in the scenario events list (see section 3.2.4). Thus, these events are forwarded directly to the *EventEvaluator* for processing.

Application-Events

In this case, we are interested in detecting events such as "the system time is 14:00" or events generated by timers. A timer is an actor type that expires at a certain point in time. This point is set when creating the timer (i.e. we can create a timer that will go off after 50 seconds). Timer events are dealt with in the same way as intra-object events. That is, each timer is paired with a *TimerListener* that waits for the timer event to happen and sends it to the *EventEvaluator* when it occurs.

Before concluding our discussion on event detection, we would like to remark that each event sent to the *EventEvaluator* is accompanied by a timestamp, indicating the exact point in time the event occurred. These timestamps are acquired by a general application timer that starts together with the scenario start relative to the IMD session start. The application timers' granularity is 1 second and indicates how many seconds have passed from the beginning of the scenario presentation.

Evaluating Events

The next step is to evaluate the events occurred so far. All detected events are simple events and they are all sent to the *EventEvaluator*. This means that on arrival of a new event, the start and stop event expressions (complex events) of all tuples should be evaluated. Those that are found to be true trigger the appropriate actions. This task may be complex since the start/stop event expressions may be arbitrarily complex, so an incremental evaluation as new events occur is necessary. The *EventEvaluator* additionally controls the synchronization of all modules that send messages to it about events that occurred. This function is further explained in the *EvaluatorNotifier* class..

Hereafter we present the *HistoryList* class, which is contained in the *EventEvaluator* class as an attribute. There is only one instance of this class in each IMD session and keeps information on the events that have occurred in an IMD session, from the start to the current time, which is defined as the time elapsed since the session start. For each event we keep all the timestamps of its occurrences. For example, the entry: <e1, 3, 6, 12> implies that event "e1" occurred 3 times with the timestamps: 3, 6 and 12. The timestamps refer to the time elapsed from the IMD session start in seconds. It is important to clarify that in the *HistoryList* only simple and tuple synchronization events that have occurred in the current IMD session, are stored. In this structure there is no information on events that are included in the *Events* list, but have not occurred up to the current moment.

Upon arrival of an event, the *EventEvaluator* locks itself (i.e. does not accept any further messages) until the event evaluation process finishes. During this process, the aim is to find all tuples that have to start or stop due to the occurrence of the current event. Once all tuples that must either start or stop have been found, the *EventEvaluator* sends the appropriate messages to the *ScenarioPlayer* to act accordingly and continues processing any synch events that these tuples may have defined. In some cases an occurring event may cause both the start and the stop event of a tuple to be evaluated as true. If this is the case, then the system allows a tuple either to start or stop, but not both. The choice is made according to the current state of the tuple.

On evaluating an event expression as TRUE, several actions may be taken such as starting/interrupting a tuple or interrupting the IMD session. The evaluation process is carried out by a set of functions that are further presented. First we are interested in the evaluation of a simple occurring event. This task is accomplished by the function evaluate_simple_event() involved each time the *EventEvaluator* receives a single event (this may be a simple event or a synchronization event). The function follows:

```
EventEvaluator "locks" itself
evaluate_simple_event(simple event e)
EventEvaluator writes e to HistoryList
for each tuple t
      if t is idle
      then
                  evaluate (t.start_event, e)
                  if t.start_event is true
                        then add t in tuples_to_start array

      else
      if t is active
            then
                        evaluate (t.stop_event, e)
                        if t.stop_event is true
                        then add t in tuples_to_stop array
start_tuples(tuples_to_start)
stop_tuples(tuples_to_stop)
EventEvaluator "unlocks" access to others
```

It is important to stress that during the period of event processing (*EventEvaluator* in locked state) the occurring events are not lost but are maintained in the respective *EvaluatorNotifiers*. When the *EventEvaluator* finishes processing an event, notifies all *EvaluatorNotifiers* that may have a new event to send, since it is now available to process a new event. It then receives a new event, falls again into the locked state and processes it. By having the *EventEvaluator* notify the *EvaluatorNotifiers* instead of having them poll the *EventEvaluator* at regular time intervals we have a significant gain in performance as the *EventEvaluator* is used as soon as it is needed.

The function evaluate(t.start_event, e) carries out the evaluation of the event e presented in more details further in this section. Hereby we present the algorithms for starting/interrupting tuples whose corresponding start/stop events were found to be true:

```
start_tuples(array tuples_to_start)
        for each  t in tuples_to_start
                ScenarioPlayer starts t
                if t.start_synch_event not null
                        then evaluate_simple_event(t.start_synch_event)

stop_tuples(array tuples_to_stop)
for each  t in tuples_to_start
                ScenarioPlayer stops t
                if t.stop_synch_event not null
                        then evaluate_simple_event(t.stop_synch_event)
```

In the sequel we will explain the way the evaluate() method works. When the start/stop event expression is a simple event, the evaluation is limited in searching in the HistoryList for an occurrence of such an event. For example, if a tuple must start when event "e2" happens, all we have to do when checking the start event expression of that tuple is to see if "e2" exists in the HistoryList.

In the case that the start/stop event expression is complex, it may contain expressions including operators and functions that are defined in the framework presented in chapter two. Our current rendering scheme implements the AND, OR and NOT operators and the functions: ANY, ANYNEW, IN, TIMES, SEQ and (event1:time interval: event2). In this case the evaluation process is carried out in three distinct steps. The first step is the transformation of the event expression into postfix form resulting in an expression without brackets. The second step is evaluating each function appearing in the expression, and replacing the function with the token "true" or "false" if this is the case. The last step is to evaluate the result of the tokens "true" or "false" combined with the Boolean operators. The above-described steps are demonstrated in the following example. Assume we are at time 13secs from the start of the scenario, we are evaluating event "e5" and we are now processing the start event expression: "(e1 AND ANY (2; e1; e2; e5)) OR e4". The contents of the *HistoryList* appear in Table 6.1.

Event	Timestamps
E1	2, 7, 12
E3	5
E5	13

Table 6.1. The contents of the History list at time 13 sec.

The *first step* will result in the transformation of the event into the expression (the symbol "/" serves as a delimiter):

e1/ANY(2;e1;e2;e5)/AND/e4/OR

The *second step* will produce the expression

"true/true/AND/false/OR"

The *third step* will evaluate this expression to "true". If the tuple with the above event expression is idle (i.e. has not already started or has already finished), then it must be started.

What would happen if we had multiple occurrences of start/stop events? Should we re-start the actions? We have dealt with this problem and we propose a mechanism that enables multiple execution of tuples in the same IMD session. Assume tuple t1, and t1.start_event = "e2 AND e3" and that event e1 occurs at time 13sec with the HistoryList being as appears in Table 6.2.

Event	Timestamps
e2	3, 9
e3	7
e1	13

Table 6.2. The contents of the History list at time 13 sec.

During the evaluation of e1, the expression "e2 AND e3" would evaluate to true, and provided that tuple t1 had finished playing, we would have to start it again. As it is clear, event e1 that is under evaluation, is irrelevant to tuple t1 and it would make no sense to start tuple t1 because of an irrelevant event.

Therefore, we have expanded the evaluation mechanism to check whether the simple event (for instance e1) we are currently processing is related to the tuple whose start or stop event expression we are evaluating. If e1 participates in the start or stop event expression, then the evaluation process goes on. Otherwise, the evaluation stops. For instance, in the above example, e1 does not participate in the expression "e2 AND e3"; thus, the expression will not be further evaluated. This mechanism enables a tuple to be executed several times as its' start event expression will become true only when the proper event occurs.

6.2.4   Starting and Interrupting Scenario Tuples

In order to accomplish this task, the client must detect and evaluate the events that occur in an IMD session and match them against the events included in the start/stop event attributes of the scenario tuples. A tuple is considered *active* when the start event of that tuple is evaluated as *true*. At this point all instruction streams of the tuple start execution at the same time, though they do not have to stop concurrently.

When an IMD session starts none of its tuples is active. A special event called "StartApp" (start application) is generated and the tuples whose start event is the "StartApp" event, start their execution. A tuple cannot be restarted when it is active, even if its' start event becomes true. A tuple can only start again once it has stopped/finished and, thus, is in idle state.

Once a tuple has been initiated there are two ways it may end: *natural* or *forced*. In the first case, the tuple falls into the idle state when all instruction streams have finished. An instruction stream state is considered as finished when all the involved actors have fallen into stopped state. In the second case, the tuple stops when its' stop event becomes true. In order to avoid confusion we explain what are the semantics of interrupting an actor. For this purpose we distinguish actors with inherent temporal features (sound or video) and actors without such features. An actor of the first category falls in the idle state either when its' natural end comes (there is no more data to be presented) or when it is stopped using the stop operator "!". Actors of the second category (e.g. an image) stop only when we apply the stop operator on them.

Hereafter we will examine the classes that are related to management of scenario tuples, namely the *ScenarioPlayer*, the *TuplePlayer*, the *EventEvaluator*, and the *HistoryList* classes.

The *ScenarioPlayer* class is responsible for the execution of an IMD. Initially it constructs the window where the media are to be presented (a "frame" in Java jargon) and becomes able to receive all input events (keyboard or mouse generated) as well as all application timer events (the entity that counts the overall application time). This class is also responsible for starting and interrupting tuples. In order to achieve these tasks the *ScenarioPlayer* maintains information about the IMD session in structures supported by a set of auxiliary classes. The most important ones are:

- *Actors*: stores information on the participating objects and their spatiotemporal transformations in the current IMD.

- *Tuples*: stores the tuples of the IMD

- *Events*: stores information about the events that the IMD will consume. It includes only the simple events, while the potentially complex events that are defined as scenario tuple start/stop or synchronization events are stored in the corresponding tuples.

- *ActorsEnabled*: stores information on the actors that are currently active together with the identifier of the tuple that activated them and their activation time, referring to the temporal start of the IMD.

- *TuplesEnabled*: stores a list with the tuples that have been activated and/or stopped during the IMD session along with the activation/interrupting time points. It is clear that a scenario tuple may be executed more than once during a session, depending on the occurring events.

The *TuplePlayer* class is in charge of starting and interrupting a scenario tuple, in other words it starts the instruction streams of the scenario tuple with no further effect on them. Each time a scenario tuple is to be started, the ScenarioPlayer creates a TuplePlayer object. When it is stopped/finished, the *TuplePlayer* must destroy the related occurrences of the *InstructionStreamPlayer* class. The *TuplePlayer* must detect the termination of the instruction streams that are included. When all instruction streams have finished, the *TuplePlayer* informs the *ScenarioPlayer*. At this point it is stopped.

6.2.5   Synchronized Presentation of Media-Objects

In this section we present the classes of the client that are in charge of presenting the media objects according to the synchronization relationships that are included in the instruction streams. As mentioned above each scenario tuple consists of a set of instruction streams. Not all instruction streams have the same effect on actor states. In this respect we distinguish two categories of instruction streams.

The first one includes instruction streams whose synchronization expression starts with an actor followed by start operator (>). These instruction streams start immediately after the tuple activation and remain active until all participating actors stop. The second category includes instruction streams that contain the synchronization operator "∧". These instruction streams also start immediately but remain active until the temporally shorter of the involved actors ends its execution. If an instruction stream contains the synchronization operator "∧", it cannot contain any other operator (i.e. >, !, ||, \>).

The *InstructionStreamPlayer* class is designed to execute an instruction stream as defined in earlier sections. The way this is done is by parsing the instruction stream string at execution time and executing the actions it says as we parse it. For example, assume the instruction stream: "video1> 4 image1> 0 button1> 5 video1||". It implies that the video clip "video1" should start, and after 4 seconds the image "image1" be presented. Immediately after the button "button1" is presented and after 5 seconds video1 is suspended.

The *InstructionStreamPlayer* will start parsing the instruction stream and will find string "video1". This string must be an actor (actually the ScenarioPlayer verifies the name, since this class maintains information about the actors). Once *InstructionStreamPlayer* gets the actor "video1", it continues parsing and finds the start operator (">") is to be applied to video1. This is accomplished by creating a new *VideoListener* object, which starts the video presentation according to the specifications of the corresponding actor. While the *VideoListener* performs this task, the *InstructionStreamPlayer* continues parsing, finding the 4 seconds pause. This is accomplished by falling in the idle state (i.e. release the CPU) for 4 seconds, and then continue parsing. The same steps (find actor, find operator, apply operator to actor, and wait for a number of seconds) are repeated until the whole instruction stream is processed. A new listener object is created only when the start operator is found. For the other operators, the *InstructionStreamPlayer* does not create a new listener; instead it sends the appropriate message (pause, resume or stop) to the corresponding listener previously created. A limitation of this approach is that it does not allow negative temporal intervals between presentation operations (i.e. "video1> -2 sound1>"). (One can very easily bypass this just by swapping the order of the actors i.e. "sound1> 2 video1>").

In the case of synchronization expressions including the operator "∧" (for example assume "video1∧ button1∧ sound2∧ text3") things are slightly different. All actors participating in the instruction stream are first inserted in an array and then the appropriate listeners are created for these actors. Each listener presents one media object and when the first objects finishes, the corresponding listener notifies the *InstructionStreamPlayer* which in turn sends messages to all the remaining listeners to stop.

In order to present single media objects, we use a set of listener classes. A set of six classes (each for a different kind of actor) were created and all have the suffix "Listener". These classes do not only present actors but also detect ("listen to") any events concerning the actor they are controlling (i.e. media state changes etc.). For instance, the *VideoListener* class can start, stop, pause and resume a video clip and can also detect all kinds of events that are related to the particular video. A *VideoListener* must receive appropriate messages to start, pause, resume and stop the video it is currently playing. The class is also in charge of presenting the video according to the specifications in the corresponding actor (i.e. volume intensity, start point, screen coordinates etc). The same applies to the other listeners, namely *SoundListener*, *ImageListener*, *TextListener*, *ButtonListener* and *LabelListener*.

Each listener occurrence is paired with an occurrence of the *EvaluatorNotifier* class. This class serves as a filtering mechanism that sends to the EventEvaluator only the events of interest to the IMD (i.e. contained in the *Scenario Events* list). The *EvaluatorNotifier* receives messages denoting actor state change, checks whether there is a related event defined in the IMD *Events* list and, if such an event exists, sends it to the *EventEvaluator*. For example, if the *ButtonListener* for button A detects that the button has been pressed, it will send a "ButtonDown" event to the *EvaluatorNotifier*. The *EvaluatorNotifier* checks if an event "ButtonDown" related to button A exists in the *Scenario Events* list. If such an event exists, it will be sent to the *EventEvaluator* together with the occurrence time (timestamp). The *EvaluatorNotifier* class is responsible for performing the filtering of events so that the EventEvaluator does not have to process redundant events.

7. Indexing Large Multimedia Applications: A Spatiotemporal Indexing Scheme

7.1   Introduction

In previous chapters introduced a model for representation of multimedia spatiotemporal compositions. Authoring complex IMDs (for instance 3D synthetic movies [Krie96]) that involve a large number of objects (typically $\geq 10^4$) may be a very complicated task, keeping in mind the large set of possible spatiotemporal relationships that may encounter in the application context. Typically in a 90minutes synthetic movie we would expect the number of objects and their relationships to be 10^4 or bigger with respect to the order of magnitude. Taking in account the vast number of possible events and their combinations based on (user and object) interaction, the amount of the entities that have to be managed by the IMD authors is considerable.

The authoring procedures presented in previous chapters provide the tools to the authors for declarative high level complete specification of the IMD. During the development of a digital movie the authors/directors would apparently submit queries related to the:

- spatial (screen) layout at a specific time instances during the movie

- the temporal layout of the movie in terms of temporal intervals

- the spatiotemporal relationships among objects (actors) (i.e., *"does object A spatially overlap with object B?"* or *"which objects temporally overlap with object A?"*)

In this chapter we propose indexing schemes (i.e., disk resident structures organizing spatiotemporal features of media objects) for large IMDs in order to provide fast response to author queries in order to manage the large number of objects, have spatial and temporal layouts of parts of or the entire application and answer queries regarding spatiotemporal relationships among objects. The proposed indexing schemes are based on the R-tree index [Gutt84] which is widely used for indexing of spatial data in several applications, such as Geographic Information Systems (GIS), CAD and VLSI design, etc. We adapt R-trees in order to index either spatial, temporal or spatiotemporal occurrences of objects and relationships between them. Moreover, we evaluate the proposed schemes each other and against two simple cases: the simplest one, based on serial storage of objects' spatiotemporal coordinates, and a slightly more sophisticated one, which keeps disk resident arrays of pre-sorted object coordinates according to each direction (i.e., lower x- or y- coordinate and start point at t- axis). We also give also hints to multimedia database designers in order to select the most efficient scheme according to the requirements of IMD authors.

In the literature there is limited previous work, according to our knowledge, on indexing spatiotemporal characteristics of IMDs. Research has mainly focused on *content-based* image indexing, i.e., fast retrieval of objects using their content characteristics (color, texture, shape). For example, in [Falo94] a system, called *QBIC*, that couples several features from machine vision with fast indexing methods from the database area is proposed in order to support color, shape and texture matching queries. Nearest-neighbor queries (based on image content) are addressed in [Chiu94]. In general, indexing of objects' contents is an active research area while indexing of objects' extends in the spatiotemporal coordinate system sets a new direction.

The chapter is organized as follows: In section two we present an example of IMD based on the spatiotemporal composition and we submit some sample queries involving spatiotemporal properties and relationships. In the next section we propose indexing schemes for IMDs: one based on sorted arrays and another based on the R-tree spatial index (a simple and a unified one), in order to support these operators. The analytical evaluation of the proposed schemes is presented in section four.

7.2   A Sample Multimedia Composition

In this section we present a sample IMD that will serve as a running example in the presentation of the spatiotemporal indexing scheme. It corresponding to TV news clip in terms of spatiotemporal relationships as defined above. The high level scenario of the application is the following:

" *The **News** clip starts with presentation of image A (located at point 50,50 relatively to the application origin Θ). At the same time a background music E starts. 10 sec after a video clip B starts. It appears to the right side (18cm) and below the upper side of A (12cm). Just after the end of B, another IMD starts. This IMD(**Fashion_clip**) is related to fashion. The Fashion_clip consists of a video clip C that showing the highlights of a fashion show and appears 7cm below (and left aligned to) the position of B. 3 sec after the start of C, a text logo D (the designer's logo) appears inside C, 8cm above the bottom side of C, aligned to the right side. D will remain for 4 sec on the screen. Meanwhile, at the 10th sec of the News clip, the TV channel logo (F) appears at the bottom-left corner of the application window. F disappears after 3 sec. The application ends when music background E ends.* "

The spatial composition (screen layout) appears in Figure 7.1, while the temporal one appears in Figure 7.2. The objects to be included in a composition tuple of a IMD, are those that are spatially and/or temporally related. In our example (News clip), A and B and Fashion clip should be in the same composition tuple since A relates to B, B relates to Fashion clip. On the other hand, F is not related to any other object, nor spatially neither temporally, so it composes a different tuple.

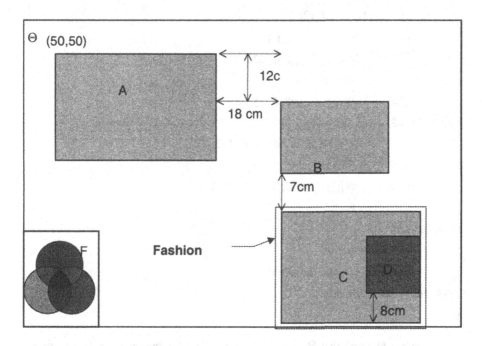

Figure 7.1. The spatial composition of the News IMD

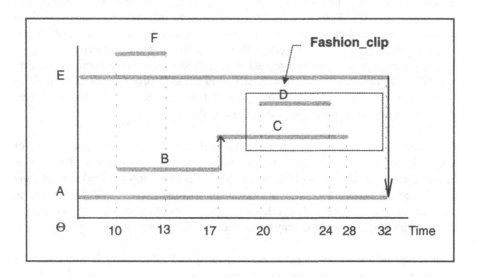

Figure 7.2. The temporal composition of the News IMD

The above spatial and temporal specifications defined by the author in a high level GUI are transformed into the following representation according to the model primitives defined in chapter two:

// News Clip

composition = {r1, r2}

$r1 = $ Θ [(_, _, _, _,_), (>0>)]

E [(_, _, _, _,_), (<0!)]

News

$r2 = $ Θ [(r1_1, _,v2, 5, 5), (>0>)]

A [(r11_13, v3, v2,18,12),(>10>)]

B [(r13_6, v1, v2, 0,-7), (>0>)]

Fashion_clip

$r3 = $ Θ [(_, _, v1, 0, 300), (>10>)]

F

// Fashion clip

composition = {r4}

$r4 = \Theta$ [(_, _,v2,0,0), (>0>)]

C [(r9_10, v4, v4, 0, 8), (>3>)]

D

It is important to stress that Θ in composition tuple $r4$ represents the spatiotemporal origin of the Fashion clip. In this example we have a composition of IMDs. It has to be stressed that when the host IMD (i.e. News_clip) ends all the IMDs started by that are stopped also (i.e. Fashion_clip). There is an issue regarding the mapping of the spatiotemporal specifications into the composition tuples: the classification of objects in composition tuples. The procedure that we propose is the following: For each object A_i we check whether it is related to objects already classified into an existing tuple. If the answer is positive, A_i is classified to the appropriate composition tuple (a procedure that possibly leads to reorganization of the tuples). Otherwise, a new composition tuple, composed by Θ and A_i, is created.

The objects to be included in a composition tuple are those that are spatially and/or temporally related to each other. During the application development process it is expectable (especially in the case of complex and large applications) that authors would need information related to the spatiotemporal features of the IMD (TV clip in the case of the example). The related queries, depending on the spatiotemporal relationships that are involved, may be classified in the following categories:

• pure spatial or temporal: only temporal or spatial relationship is involved. For instance: *"which objects temporally overlap the presentation of test logo D?"* , *"which objects spatially lie above object D in the application window?"*,

- spatiotemporal: where such a relationship is involved. For instance: *"which objects spatially overlap with object D during its presentation?"*.

- layout, : related to the spatial or temporal layout of the application. For instance: *"what is the screen layout on the 22nd sec of the application?"*, *"which objects are presented between the 10th and the 20th sec of the application?"* (temporal layout).

A simple serial storage scheme which includes objects' spatial and temporal coordinates is an inefficient solution since typical IMDs include thousands of objects. Hence indexing techniques that could be able to efficiently handle spatial and temporal characteristics of objects need to be adopted. In the next section we propose such efficient indexing mechanisms in order to support queries lie the above ones in a large IMD.

As discussed in previous sections, IMDs usually involve a large amount of media objects, such as images, video, sound, and text. The quick retrieval of a qualifying set, among the huge amount of data, that satisfies a query based on spatiotemporal relationships is necessary for the efficient construction of an IMD. Spatial and temporal features of objects are identified by six coordinates: the projections on x- (points x_1, x_2), y- (points y_1, y_2), and t- (points t_1, t_2) axes[1]. It is not an efficient solution a serial storage scheme, maintaining the objects characteristics as a set of seven values (id, x_1, x_2, y_1, y_2, t_1, t_2) and organizing them into disk pages, since the lack of ordering leads to the access of all pages for answering any query, like the example queries of section two. However, this scheme will be used as the baseline for the evaluation of our proposals in the following sections.

A more efficient but still simplified solution (as will be presented next) is based on the maintenance of three disk arrays that keep low coordinates of objects (i.e., x_1, y_1, and t_1) separately in a sorted order[2].

7.3   Indexing Schemes

Several queries involving spatiotemporal operators, require the retrieval of one array only, using "divide-and-conquer" techniques. Temporal layout queries (such as query 5) belong to this group. However, the majority of queries involve information about

---

[1] We adopt a unified three-dimensional context for space (two dimensions) and time (one dimension) features.

[2] Instead of using low- coordinates one can select high- coordinates (or six arrays with low- and high-coordinates). It is a decision that does not affect the discussion that will follow and its conclusions.

more than one axis. Hence the retrieval of more than one arrays and the subsequent combination of the answer sets is necessary for such cases. As a conclusion, efficient indexing mechanisms that could combine spatiotemporal characteristics of objects in order to efficiently support a wide range of spatiotemporal operators need to be present in an IMD authoring tool. In the next subsections we propose two indexing schemes and their retrieval procedures.

7.3.1   A Simple Spatial and Temporal Indexing Scheme

A simple indexing scheme that could be able to handle spatial and temporal characteristics of media objects consists of two indexes:

- a *spatial (two-dimensional) index*: for spatial characteristics (id, and x_1, x_2, y_1, y_2 values) of the objects, and

- a *temporal index*:for temporal characteristics (id, and t_1, t_2 values) of the objects.

In the literature concerning the area of *spatial databases*:, several data structures have been proposed for the manipulation of spatial data (a survey can be found in [Same90]). Among others, R-trees [Gutt84] and their variants [Sell87, Beck90] seem to be the most efficient ones. On the other hand, the manipulation of temporal information can be supported either by one-dimensional versions of the above data structures (since all of them have been designed for n-dimensional space in general) or by specialized temporal data structures, such as Segment Trees [Bent75] or Segment R-trees [Kolo91].

For uniformity reasons we select a single multi-dimensional data structure (R-tree): to play the role of the spatial (2D R-tree) and temporal (1D R-tree) index. The above indexing scheme is illustrated in Figure 7.3. The R-tree [Gut84] is a height-balanced tree, which consists of intermediate and leaf nodes. A *leaf node* is of the form

$$(oid, RECT)$$

where *oid* is an object identifier and is used to refer to an object in the database. *RECT* is the MBR (<u>M</u>inimum <u>B</u>ounding <u>R</u>ectangle) approximation of the data object, i.e., it is of the form

$$(p_{l\text{-}1}, p_{l\text{-}2}, \dots, p_{l\text{-}n}, p_{u\text{-}1}, p_{u\text{-}2}, \dots, p_{u\text{-}n})$$

which represents the $2n$ coordinates of the lower-left (p_l) and the upper-right (p_u) corner of a n-dimensional (hyper-) rectangle p. An *intermediate node* is of the form

$$(ptr, RECT)$$

where *ptr* is a pointer to a lower level node of the tree and *RECT* is a representation of the rectangle that encloses.

In our case R-tree is implemented in ANSI C under the UNIX operating system. Currently R-tree is integrated in commercial DBMSs like ILLUSTRA [Ubel94]. In the case of other systems (like ORACLE, SYBASE etc.) the R-tree code cannot be integrated, thus an interface layer should be implemented so that the index data communicate with the data base data. As regards performance, in principle, the architecture is not affecting the performance since R-tree is a disk resident structure and the only factor that is taken into account for estimating performance is the number of disk accesses.

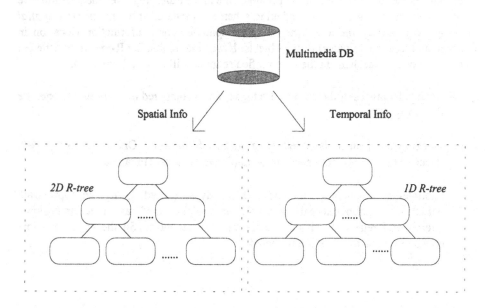

Figure 7.3. A simple (spatial and temporal) indexing scheme

We argue that the adoption of the above indexing scheme improves the retrieval of spatiotemporal operators compared to the "sorted arrays" scheme. Even for complex operators where both tree indexes need to be accessed (e.g. for the *overlap_during* operator) the cost of the two indexes' response times is expected to be lower than the retrieval cost of the (three) arrays.

A weak point of the above scheme has been already mentioned. The retrieval of objects according to their spatiotemporal relationships (e.g. the *overlap_during* one) with others, demands access to both indexes and, in a second phase, the computation of the intersection set between the two answer sets. Access to both indexes is usually costly and, in many cases, most of the elements of the two answer sets are not found in the intersection set. In other words, most of the disk accesses to each index separately are useless. To eliminate this problem, several techniques for *spatial join:*, between two R-trees for example, have been proposed [Brin93] and could be applied to our indexing scheme. However, this solution is not applicable when two completely different indexes are used (e.g. an R-tree for spatial information and a Segment Tree for temporal information). A more efficient solution is the merging of the two indexes (the spatial and the temporal one) in a unified mechanism. This scheme is proposed in the next subsection.

7.3.2   A Unified Spatiotemporal Indexing Scheme

In this subsection we propose a unified spatiotemporal indexing scheme that eliminates the inefficiencies of the previous one and further improves the performance of an IMD tool. The proposed indexing scheme consists of only one index: a *spatial (three-dimensional) index* for the complete spatiotemporal information (location in space and time coordinates) of the objects. If we assume that the R-tree is an efficient spatial indexing mechanism then the unified scheme is illustrated Figure 7.4.

The main advantages of the proposed scheme, when compared to the previous one, are the following:

- Indexing mechanism is based on a unified framework. Only one spatial data structure (e.g. the R-tree) needs to be implemented and maintained.

- Spatiotemporal operators are more efficiently supported. Using the appropriate definitions, spatiotemporal operators are implemented as three-dimensional queries and retrieved using the three-dimensional index. So the need for (time consuming) spatial joins is eliminated.

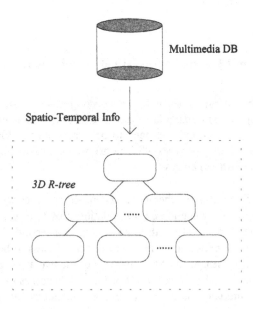

Figure 7.4. A unified (spatiotemporal) indexing scheme

The evaluation of the two proposed indexing schemes against each other and against the "sorted-arrays" and the serial storage ones will be presented in later sections where analytical models that predict the performance of each scheme will be presented. In the rest of the section we will describe the retrieval process of such operators when the unified indexing scheme is available within an IMD authoring tool.

7.3.3   Retrieval of Spatiotemporal Operators Using R-trees

The majority of multi-dimensional data structures have been designed as extensions of the classic alphanumeric index, B-tree [Come79]. They usually divide the plane into appropriate sub-regions and store these sub-regions in hierarchical tree structures. Objects are represented in the tree structure by an approximation (the MBR approximation being the most common one) instead of their actual scheme, for simplicity and efficiency reasons.

Unfortunately, relative position of two MBRs does not convey full information about the spatial (topological, direction, distance) relationship between the actual objects. For this reason, spatial queries involve the following two-step strategy [Oren86]:

- *Filter step*: The tree structure is used to rapidly eliminate objects that could not possibly satisfy the query. The result of this step is a set of candidates which includes all the results and possibly some false hits.

- *Refinement step*: Each candidate is examined (by using computational geometry techniques). False hits are detected and eliminated.

R-tree [Gutt84] is one of the most efficient hierarchical multi-dimensional data structures. It is a height-balanced tree, which consists of intermediate and leaf nodes (stored in secondary memory as disk pages). The MBRs of the actual data objects are assumed to be stored in the leaf nodes of the tree. Intermediate nodes are built by grouping rectangles (or hyper-rectangles, in general) at the lower level. An intermediate node is associated with some rectangle, which encloses all rectangles that correspond to lower level nodes. In order to retrieve objects that belong to the answer set of a spatiotemporal operator, with respect to a reference object, we have to specify the MBRs that could enclose such objects and then to search the intermediate nodes that contains these MBRs.

As an example, Figure 7.5.b shows how the MBRs corresponding to the presentations of the objects are grouped and stored in the 3D R-tree of our unified scheme. We assume a branching factor of 4, i.e., each node contains at most four entries. At the lower level, MBRs of objects are grouped into two nodes R1 and R2, which in turn compose the root of the index. If we consider the query of section two corresponding to the *overlap_during* operator with D being the reference object *q*. In order to answer this query, only R2 is selected for propagation. Among the entries of R2, objects C and (obviously) D are the ones that constitute the qualified answer set.

Note that only the right subtree of the R-tree index of Figure 7.5.a was propagated in order to answer the query. The rate of the accessed nodes heavily depends on the size of the reference object q and, of course, the kind of the operator (more selective operators result to smaller number of accessed nodes).

If we now consider the queries of section two, corresponding to the *overlap* operator with D being the reference object q. Because the query gives no temporal information on the reference object, the unified scheme transforms it to a large cube that covers the whole t- axis. In this case, the simple scheme, presented in previous subsection, could be more efficient, since the 2D R-tree that is dedicated to spatial information of objects is able to answer the query. Similarly, the queries corresponding to the *during* operator and could also be efficiently supported by the simple scheme.

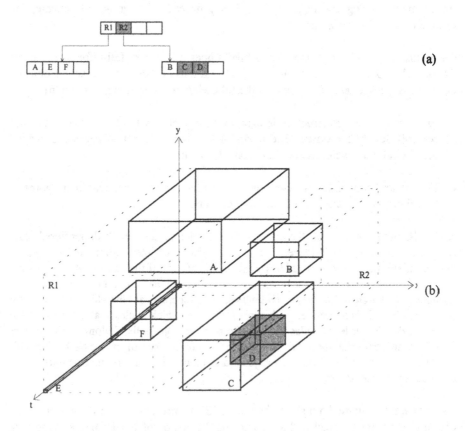

(a)

(b)

Figure 7.5. Retrieval of *overlap_during* operator using 3D R-trees

A special type of queries, which is very popular during IMD authoring, consists of *spatial* or *temporal* layout: retrieval. In other words, queries of the type *"Find the objects and their position in screen at the T_0 second"* (spatial layout) or *"Find the objects that appear in the application during the (T_1, T_2) temporal segment and their* *temporal duration*" (temporal layout) need to be supported by the underlying scheme. As we will present next, both types of queries are efficiently supported by the unified scheme, since they correspond to the *overlap_during* operator and an appropriate reference object q: a rectangle q_1 that intersects t-axis at point T_0, or a cube q_2 that overlaps t-axis at the (T_1, T_2) segment, respectively. The reference objects q_1 and q_2 are illustrated in Figure 7.6.a. In a second step the objects that compose the answer set are filtered in main memory in order to design their positions on the screen (spatial layout) or the intersection of their t- projections to the given temporal segment (temporal layout).

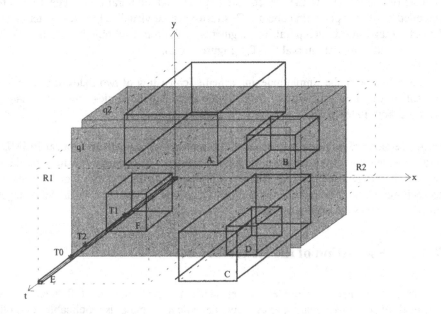

(a) query windows for spatial and temporal layout

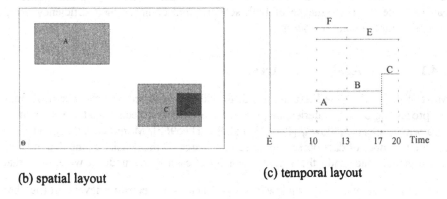

(b) spatial layout

(c) temporal layout

Figure 7.6. Spatial and temporal layout retrieval using 3D R-trees

The queries of section two corresponding to the "layout" type queries could be processed as described above. In particular, the spatial layout query could be answered by exploiting the reference object q_1 at the specific time instance $T_0 = 22sec$. The result would be a list of objects (the identifiers of the objects, their spatial and temporal coordinates) that are displayed at that temporal instance on the screen. This result may be visualized as a screen snapshot, with the objects that are included in the answer set drawn in that (Figure 7.6.b). As for the temporal layout query, it could be answered using as reference object a cube q_2 having dimensions $(X_{max}-0) \cdot (Y_{max}-0) \cdot (T_2-T_1)$ where $X_{max} \cdot Y_{max}$ is the dimension of the screen and (T_2-T_1) is the requested temporal interval; $T_1 = 10$ and $T_2 = 20$ in our example. The result would be a list of objects (the identifiers of the objects, their spatial and temporal coordinates) that are included or overlapped with cube q_2. This result can be visualized towards a temporal layout by drawing the temporal line segments of the retrieved objects that lie within the requested temporal interval (T_2-T_1) (Figure 7.6.c).

On the other hand, the simple indexing scheme (consisting of two index structures) is not able to give straightforward answers to the above layout queries, since information stored in both indexes needs to be retrieved and combined.

In this section we proposed two schemes for indexing of objects that appear in IMDs and presented the retrieval procedure that concerns spatiotemporal operators on these objects. In the next section both schemes will be analytically evaluated and compared to each other. Their comparison will result to general conclusions on the advantages and disadvantages of each solution.

7.4   Estimation of the Retrieval Cost

We present an analytical model that estimates the performance of R-trees on the retrieval of n-dimensional queries. The analytical formula is applicable to both indexing schemes, if we keep in mind that the simple one consists of one 2D R-tree and one 1D R-tree while the unified one consists of one 3D tree. Using this model we can estimate the performance of both schemes and compare their efficiency using several spatiotemporal operators.

7.4.1   Cost Analysis of R-trees

Most of the work in the literature has dealt with the expected performance of R-trees for processing *overlap* queries, i.e., the retrieval of data objects p that share common area with a query window q [Page93, Falo94, Theo96b]. More particularly, let N be the total number of data objects indexed in a R-tree, D the density of the data objects in the global space and f the average capacity of each R-tree node. If we assume that the average size of a query window q is $\prod_{i=1}^{n} q_i$ then the expected retrieval cost (number of disk accesses) of an *overlap* query using R-trees is [Theo96b]:

$$C(q) = 1 + \sum_{j=1}^{1+\left\lceil \log_f \frac{N}{f} \right\rceil} \left\{ \frac{N}{f^j} \cdot \prod_{i=1}^{n} \left(\left(D_j \cdot \frac{f^j}{N} \right)^{1/n} + q_i \right) \right\} \quad (1)$$

where the average density of the R-tree nodes D_j at each level j is given by:

$$D_j = \left\{ 1 + \frac{(D_{j-1})^{1/n} - 1}{f^{1/n}} \right\}^n \quad (2)$$

In other words, D_j can be computed recursively using D_0 which denotes the density D of the data MBRs. Qualitatively, this means that we can estimate the retrieval cost of an *overlap* query based on the knowledge of the data set and the query window only.

Since Eq. 1 expresses the expected performance of R-trees on *overlap* queries using a query window q, in order to estimate the retrieval cost of a spatiotemporal operator R(p,q) we need the following transformation: R(p,q) $\Rightarrow$ overlap(p,Q). In other words, the retrieval of a spatiotemporal operator using R-trees is equivalent (in terms of cost) to the retrieval of an *overlap* query using an appropriate query window Q. The necessary transformation Q for each operator R should take into consideration the corresponding constraint of the intermediate nodes, since only these nodes are important when estimating the retrieval cost [Papa95]. For the spatiotemporal operators that we consider in this paper, the appropriate query windows Q are illustrated in Figure 7.7. Figure 7.7.a illustrates query windows Q (3D boxes) with respect to the eight operators discussed, while Figure 7.7.b and Figure 7.7.c illustrate query windows Q (2D rectangles and 1D line segments, respectively) that correspond to spatial (*overlap*, *above*) and temporal operators (*during*, *before*), respectively.

Using information from Figure 7.7 and Eq. 1 we can estimate the expected cost for the query window *Q*, which equals to the expected cost *C(R)* for the retrieval of a spatiotemporal operator *R*. The accuracy of the above analytical model has been already evaluated on spatial relationships of varying selectivity (e.g., *inside*, *near*, *northeast*, and combinations) in [Theo95]. Intuitively, we assume that the unified scheme should be the most efficient solution when both spatial and temporal information are included in the query while in the rest cases the simple scheme seems to be preferable. The accuracy of these intuitive conclusions will be examined in the next subsection where the above analytical model will be used as a basis for the analytical comparison of the proposed schemes.

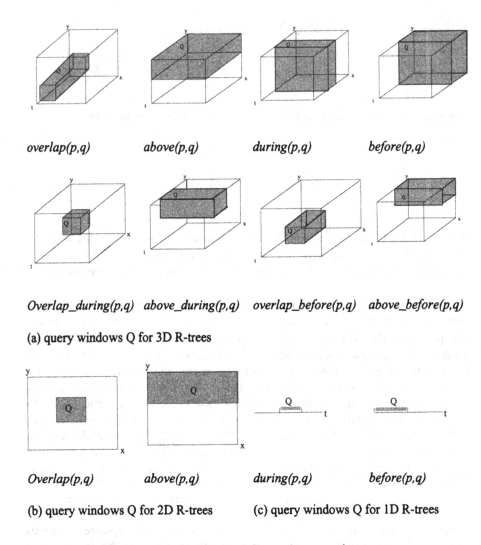

Figure 7.7. Query windows Q for spatiotemporal operators

7.4.2   Analytical Comparison of the Indexing Schemes

In order to compare the efficiency of each scheme on the retrieval of spatiotemporal operators we assumed an IMD including 10,000 objects of the following distribution:

- A portion of 75% characterized by small projections on the three axes (x-, y-, t-) e.g. text or video that cover a small space on the screen and last a short time interval,

- A portion of 15% characterized by zero projection on the two axes (x-, y-) and small projection on the third axis (t-) e.g. sounds that cover zero space on the screen and last a short time interval,

- A portion of 5% characterized by small projections on the two axes (x-, y-) and large projection on the third axis (t-) e.g. heading titles or logos that cover a small space on the screen and last a long time interval, and

- A portion of 5% characterized by large projections on the two axes (x-, y-) and small projection on the third axis (t-) e.g. full text or background patterns that cover a large space on the screen and last a short time interval.

The above distribution characterizes, in general terms, a typical IMD and will be used as the sample for the comparison of the two indexing schemes. Different distributions of objects are also supported in a similar way by adapting their density D.

For the analytical estimates we used Eq. 1 and the following values: amount of data objects $N = 10,000$ (8,500) for the 1D and 3D (2D) R-tree indexes, density of data objects $D = 145, 145, 1.6$ for the 1D, 2D, and 3D indexes, respectively, and average node capacity $f = 0.67 \cdot M$, where $M = 84, 50, 35$ for 1D, 2D, and 3D R-trees, respectively[3]. The sizes of the reference objects q varied from 0% up to 50% of the global space per axis. Figure 7.8 summarizes the comparative results for the operators discussed in the paper. For uniformity reasons we set the cost of serial retrieval to be 100% and express the costs of the "sorted-arrays" scheme and the indexing schemes proposed in section three as portions of that value.

The cost of serial retrieval is computed as follows: Each object representation requires a space of 28 bytes (4 bytes X 7 numbers). If we set the size of a disk page to be 1024 bytes then a page contains 36 (= 1024 / 28) objects. Hence 278 pages are required to store 10,000 objects. All of these pages should be accessed in order to answer any spatiotemporal operator.

The cost of the "sorted-arrays" scheme is computed as follows: The scheme consists of three arrays that contain the id plus the low- (as primary key) and high- (as secondary key) coordinate of each object per axis. Hence each object representation requires a space of 12 bytes (4 bytes X 3 numbers). Since a page of 1024 bytes

---

[3]The amount of data objects stored in the 2D index is less than the ones stored in the 1D and 3D indexes because zero-space objects (e.g. sounds) are not included in the dataset of the 2D index. The D values are implied from the above distribution if we assume that small (large) space corresponds to 5% (50%) of the screen and short (long) period of time corresponds to 1% (10%) of the whole duration of the application. The 67% capacity is a typical value for R-trees and variants while the M values represent the maximum node capacity for pages of 1024 bytes.

contains 85 (= 1024 / 12) objects, each array includes 118 (= 10,000 / 85) pages. The retrieval cost per operator is a ratio of the total amount of 118 pages. This cost is computed by using classic "divide-and-conquer" techniques with respect to the constraints that characterize each operator (i.e., logarithmic cost per array for selective almost exact match queries, such as during and about 50% of the total cost per array for non-selective queries, such as overlap, above before, etc.).

The costs of the indexing schemes have been already discussed with Eq. 1 being used for their computation.

Operator	"sorted-arrays" scheme	Simple scheme (one 1D plus one 2D R-tree)	Unified scheme (one 3D R-tree)
overlap	40% - 45%	5% - 10%	5% - 15%
above	20% - 25%	45% - 50%	80% - 95%
during	1%	2% - 10%	25% - 45%
before	20% - 25%	25% - 35%	80% - 95%
overlap_during	40% - 45%	5% - 20%	1% - 5%
overlap_before	60% - 70%	35% - 40%	3% - 10%
above_during	20% - 25%	55% - 60%	15% - 25%
above_before	40% - 50%	70% - 85%	50% - 65%

Table 7.1. Comparison of indexing schemes (with respect to serial storage cost)

Several conclusions arise from the analytical comparison results presented in Table 7.1 and Figure 7.8:

- The intuitive conclusion that the simple R-tree scheme would outperform the unified one when dealing with operators that keep only temporal or spatial information while the opposite would be the case for spatiotemporal operators is really true. The first four operators are more efficiently supported by the simple scheme while the cost of the unified scheme is usually two or three times higher. The reverse situation appears for the last four operators.

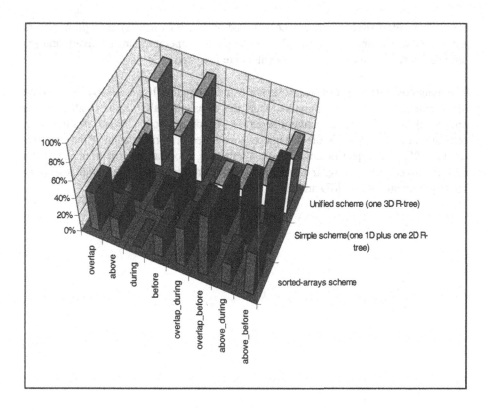

Figure 7.8. Comparison of the retrieval cost of the three indexing schemes (% of the serial storage cost)

- Both schemes based on R-trees are much more efficient than the serial storage scheme for all operators. For the most selective ones (*overlap*, *during*, *overlap_during*) the improvement is at a level of one or even two orders of magnitude, compared to the serial cost. For the least selective ones (*above*, *before*, *above_before*) the cost of the most efficient scheme is a 1/4 up to a 1/2 portion of the serial cost.

- The "sorted-arrays" scheme is shown to be a competitive solution. It always outperforms the serial storage scheme (its cost being usually a 1/5 up to a 3/5 portion of the serial cost). In comparison with the two indexing schemes based on R-trees, it is the winner when operators of very low selectivity (*above*, *before*, *above_before*) are involved while for the rest cases it remains an efficient alternative solution.

The above conclusions are, more or less, expected. However, in real cases, a mixture of temporal, spatial and spatiotemporal operators needs to be supported. The question of the most efficient scheme for such mixed requirements arises. To propose guidelines for answering this question we have presented in [Theo96a]. The average costs of the alternative indexing scheme based on R-trees when (a) all eight operators are involved, (b) only the most selective (*inclusive*) operators are involved, and (c) only the least selective (*exclusive*) operators are involved.

The main conclusion from that discussion is the following: If we distinguish between high- and low- selective operators, then the thresholds shift right (high-selective operators) or left (low-selective operators). In other words, when dealing with selective operators, the simple scheme is sometimes preferable even if the majority (up to 65%) of the queries involves spatiotemporal information. It is a choice of the multimedia database designer to select the most preferable solution, with respect to the requirements of the IMD author.

APPENDIX A: IMD Scenario Script, a Sample Application

Let us assume we want to create a presentation related to ancient Olympic Games. We have a set of related media objects ("actors") that we want to combine for the sake of the presentation. The media objects are presented according to spatial and temporal transformations and specifications according to author requirements. This conveys the spatial and temporal coordinates of the objects in the presentation context as well as their transformations under which they would be included in the presentation. These transformations are formally described in [V96]. The actor specifications appear in Table A.1.

ACTOR LABELBTN	ACTOR INTRO	ACTOR IMG1_1
Type of actor = BUTTON	Type of actor = WAVE	Type of actor = BMP
Type of button = Label	FileName = INTRO.WAV	FileName =
Caption =	Start = 0	AFI92_04.BMP
OLYMPIC GAMES	Duration = 46874	Height = 1500
Height = 1200	Volume = 100	Width = 2500
Width = 5000	Looping = No	Xcoord = 5500
Xcoord = 1500	Direction = Forward	Ycoord = 500
Ycoord = 0	Effect = None	Layer = 1
Transparent = True		PreEffect = Blinds Slow
FontFace = HellasTimes		PostEffect x= None
FontSize = 28		
Color = 255,255,0		
FontStyle =		
Bold,Italic,Underline		
ACTOR IMG1_2	ACTOR IMG1_3	ACTOR RUNS
Type of actor = BMP	Type of actor = BMP	Type of actor = AVI
FileName =	FileName =	FileName =
32_169_1.BMP	MB_1511.BMP	OPLODROM.AVI
Height = 1800	Height = 3500	Start = 0
Width = 2500	Width = 3000	Duration = 1667
Xcoord = 5500	Xcoord = 500	Scale Factor = 3
Ycoord = 1400	Ycoord = 1000	Volume = 70
Layer = 1	Layer = 1	Looping = Yes
PreEffect = Vertical Split	PreEffect = Push to	Direction = Forward
Out Normal	Top Normal	Height = 3000
PostEffect = Dissolve Fast	PostEffect = Push to	Width = 4000
	Top Normal	Xcoord = 2500
		Ycoord = 2000

ACTOR IMG2_1	ACTOR IMG2_2	ACTOR KAVALAR
Type of actor = BMP	Type of actor = BMP	Type of actor = AVI
FileName =	FileName =	FileName = KAVALAR.AVI
32_167_1.BMP	32_166_1.BMP	Start = 291
Height = 3500	Height = 2500	Duration = 1709
Width = 2500	Width = 2500	Scale Factor = 3
Xcoord = 500	Xcoord = 4500	Volume = 70
Ycoord = 1400	Ycoord = 4000	Looping = Yes
Layer = 1	Layer = 1	Direction = Forward
PreEffect = Puzzle Slow	PreEffect = Slide Out	Height = 3500
PostEffect = Dissolve Fast	Top Slow	Width = 3000
	PostEffect = Dissolve	Xcoord = 500
	Fast	Ycoord = 1000
ACTOR INFOTXT	ACTOR NEXTBTN	ACTOR EXITBTN
Type of actor = TXT	Type of actor = BUTTON	Type of actor = BUTTON
FileName =	Type of button =	Type of button =
OLYMPIC1.TXT	PushButton	PushButton
Height = 4000	Caption = Next >	Caption = Exit
Width = 4000	Height = 500	Height = 500
Xcoord = 5000	Width = 1500	Width = 1500
Ycoord = 500	Xcoord = 5000	Xcoord = 7000
Transparent = True	Ycoord = 5500	Ycoord = 5500
Layer = 1	Transparent = False	Transparent = False
BorderStyle = scrolling	FontFace = MS Sans	FontFace = MS Sans
FontFace = HellasArial	Serif	Serif
FontSize = 12	FontSize = 14	FontSize = 14
Color = 255,255,255	Color = 255,0,0	Color = 255,0,0
FontStyle = Regular	FontStyle = Bold	FontStyle = Bold
ACTOR ACDDM	ACTOR FLUTE	ACTOR IMG3_1
Type of actor = WAVE	Type of actor = WAVE	Type of actor = BMP
FileName =	FileName =	FileName =
ACDMC2M1.WAV	S_FLUTE.WAV	AFI92_03.BMP
Start = 0	Start = 0	Height = 1500
Duration = 10961	Duration = 8734	Width = 2500
Volume = 70	Volume = 90	Xcoord = 5500
Looping = No	Looping = Yes	Ycoord = 3000
Direction = Forward	Direction = Forward	Layer = 1
Effect = None	Effect = None	PreEffect =Blinds Slow
		PostEffect = None
ACTOR YMNOS	ACTOR TIMER1	
Type of actor = TXT	Type of actor =	
FileName = YMNOS.TXT	TIMER	
Height = 5800	Type of timer = Sec	
Width = 3500	(12000)	
Xcoord = 300		
Ycoord = 500		
Transparent = False		
Layer = 1		
BorderStyle = raised		
FontFace = HellasArc		
FontSize = 10		
Color = 128,0,128		
FontStyle = Italic		

Table A.1. Actors list

As mentioned above, the carriers of interactions on our model are the events (atomic or complex). Hereafter we refer to the events that the sample presentation will detect and consume. They are the following:

- DoubleClick raised when the user makes a mouse double click;

- KeyEsc raised when the user presses the key "Escape";

- IntroStop raised each time the audio clip "INTRO" ends its playback;

- ExitEvent raised each time the user presses the button "EXITBTN";

- TIMEINST raised each time the timer "TIMER1" reaches the 50th second;

- AppTimerEvent raised each time the Application timer reaches the time 02min and 30 seconds;

- ACDSoundStop raised each time the audio clip "ACDDM" stops;

- NextBtnClick: raised each time the user presses the button "NEXTBTN".

The events are formally defined in Table A.2. Having the media objects available we may build the application for the following scenario:

" The application starts (event StartApp) with presentation of button LABELBTN immediately followed by the audio clip INTRO. After 3 seconds the image IMG2_1 is presented followed by IMG2_2 after 2 seconds. After 2 more seconds the image IMG1_2 is presented at position, while after 2 seconds IMG2_1, IMG2_2 and IMG1_2 stop their presentation while after a second the video clip RUNS starts. This sequence of presentation actions may be interrupted whenever one of the events: _DoubleClick, _KeyEsc, _IntroStop occurs.

Another set of presentations ("Stage2A") starts when the event _IntroStop is raised. The presentation actions that take place are presentation of image IMG1_3 in parallel with audio clip ACDDM (when the clip ends the image disappears). In parallel, two seconds after timer TIMER1 (that started when "Stage 2A" started) expires, the text INFOTXT is presented.

The next set of media presentations ("Stage 2B") is initiated when the sequence of events _IntroStop and _ACDSoundStop occurs. During Stage2b the video clip KAVALAR starts playback while the buttons NEXTBTN and EXITBTN are presented. The presentation actions are interrupted when any of the events _TIMEINST and _NextBtnClick occurs. The end of "Stage2b" raises the synchronization event _e1.

The following set of media presentations ("Stage3") starts when any two of the events _e1, _NextBtnClick, _TIMEINST occur. During "Stage3" the text INFOTXT disappears, just after the text YMNOS appears while the audio clip FLUTE starts while two seconds after image IMG1_1 and IMG3_1 appear. Three seconds after the EXITBTN appears.

The last part of the scenario handles the presentation termination which will occur when either the _ExitEvent An application timer limits the duration of the scenario through the _AppTimer event".

The scenario is formally described in Table A.3. For each of the sentences above, a tuple is specified, providing for each tuple the start and stop events, the action list and the synchronization events.

All the specifications that appear in the following tables are results of the authoring procedure for the example introduced in chapter 4. The specifications are given according to the model introduced in [V96] and include the actors (the objects that participate in the IMD along with their spatiotemporal transformations), the events and the scenario tuples.

EVENT
_DoubleClick
    Subject = Mouse
    Action =
    DoubleClick
	EVENT _KeyEsc
	    Subject = Keyboard
	    Action = Escape
		EVENT _IntroStop
		    Subject = INTRO
		    Action = stop

EVENT _ExitEvent
    Subject = EXITBTN
    Action = click
	EVENT _TIMEINST
	    Subject = TIMER1
	    Action =
	    time_instance(50)
		EVENT _AppTimerEvent
		    Subject = ApplicationTimer
		    Action =
		    time_instance(02:30)

EVENT
_ACDSoundStop
    Subject = ACDDM
    Action = stop
	EVENT _NextBtnClick
	    Subject = NEXTBTN
	    Action = click	

Table A.2: Events list

TUPLE ExitTuple
Start Event = _ExitEvent I _AppTimerEvent Stop Event = Action List = ExitApplication Start Synch Event = None Stop Synch Event = None
TUPLE Stage1

Start Event = StartApp
Stop Event = ANYNEW(1;_DoubleClick;_KeyEsc;_IntroStop)
Action List = LABELBTN> 0 INTRO> 3 IMG2_1> 2 IMG2_2> 2
                  IMG1_2> 2 IMG2_1< 0 IMG2_2< 0 IMG1_2< 1
                  RUNS>
Start Synch Event = None
Stop Synch Event = None

TUPLE Stage2A
Start Event = _IntroStop Stop Event = Action List = (IMG1_3 ∧ACDDM) :   ($> 0 TIMER1> 2 INFOTXT>) Start Synch Event = None Stop Synch Event = None

```
TUPLE  Stage2B
   Start Event =  SEQ(_IntroStop;_ACDSoundStop)
   Stop Event =  ANY (1;_TIMEINST;_NextBtnClick)
   Action List  =  KAVALAR> 0 NEXTBTN> 0 EXITBTN>
   Start Synch Event =  None
   Stop Synch Event = _e1
TUPLE  Stage3
   Start Event =  ANY(2;_e1;_NextBtnClick;_TIMEINST)
   Stop Event =
   Action List  =  $> 0 INFOTXT< 0 FLUTE> 0 YMNOS> 2
                      IMG1_1> 0 IMG3_1> 3 EXITBTN>
   Start Synch Event =  None
   Stop Synch Event = None
```

Table A.3: Tuple list

APPENDIX B: Scenario Model, the BNF Grammar

```
scenario    ::= actor_list event_list tuple_list

actor_list ::= actor

           |  actor actor_list

event_list ::= event

           |  event event_list

tuple_list ::= tuple

           |  tuple tuple_list

actor           ::= "ACTOR"

                    actor_name

                    actor_type

                    ( actor_attributes | e )

actor_name    ::= string

actor_type    ::= "AVI" | "MPEG" | "JPG" | "GIF" | "LABEL"

              | "WAVE" | "AU" | "TXT" | "BUTTON" | "TIMER"

actor_attributes ::= video_attributes

               |  image_attributes

               |  sound_attributes

               |  text_attributes

               |  button_attributes
```

###

```
video_attributes   ::= file_attributes

                       continuous_attributes

                       visible_attributes

                       scale

image_attributes   ::= file_attributes

                       visible_attributes

                       layer

                       image_effects

sound_attributes   ::= file_attributes

                       continuous_attributes

                       sound_effect

text_attributes    ::= file_attributes

                       visible_attributes

                       textual_attributes

                       border_style

                       layer

button_attributes  ::= visible_attributes

                       textual_attributes

                       caption

file_attributes ::= file_name

                    path_name

file_name       ::= "FileName" "=" string

path_name       ::= "PathName" "=" string
```

##

```
continuous_attributes ::= start_point

                          duration

                          volume

                          looping

                          direction

start_point             ::= "Start" "=" number

duration                ::= "Duration" "=" number

volume                  ::= "Volume" "=" number

looping                 ::= "Looping" "=" ( "Yes" | "No" )

direction               ::= "Direction" "="

                            ( "Forward" | "Backward" )
```

###

```
visible_attributes ::= height

                       width

                       xcoord

                       ycoord


height                  ::= "Height" "=" number

width                   ::= "Width"  "=" number

xcoord                  ::= "Xcoord" "=" number

ycoord                  ::= "Ycoord" "=" number
```

###

```
textual_attributes ::= transparency

                       layer

                       font_face

                       font_size

                       font_style

                       color

transparency       ::= "Transparent" "="( "True" |"False" )

layer              ::= positive_number

font_face          ::= "FontFace" "=" string

font_size          ::= "FontSize" "=" positive_number

font_style         ::= "FontStyle" "="

                       ( "Regular" | "Bold" | "Italics" )

color              ::= number "," number "," number

######################################################

scale              ::= "Scale Factor" "=" number

                                   ( ("." number) | e )

image_effects ::= pre_effect

                  post_effect

pre_effect         ::= "PreEffect" "=" string

post_effect        ::= "PostEffect" "=" string

sound_effect       ::= "Effect" "=" string

caption            ::= "Caption" "=" string

border_style       ::= "BorderStyle" "=" string

######################################################
```

```
event           ::= event_name

                    subject

                    action

                    object

                    signature

event_name      ::= string

subject         ::= actor_name

                |   "Keyboard"

                |   "Mouse"

action          ::= standard_action

                |   keyboard_char

standard_action ::=   "Start"   |   "Stop"   |   "Click"   |
                      "DoubleClick"  |   "Pause"  | number

keyboard_char   ::= character

                |  "F1" | "F2" | "F3" |"F4" |"F5" |"F6"

                |  "F7" | "F8" | "F9" |"F10" |"F11" |"F12"

                |  "Escape"

object          ::= actor_name

signature       ::= string

tuple           ::= tuple_name

                    start_event

                    stop_event

                    action_list

                    start_synch_event

                    stop_synch_event

tuple_name      ::= string
```

```
start_event         ::= event_expression

stop_event          ::= (event_expression | e)

action_list         ::= instruction_stream

                      | "(" instruction_stream ")"

                    ( ";" "(" instruction_stream ")" )+

start_synch_event ::= (string | "None")

stop_synch_event  ::= (string | "None")
```

##

```
event_expression    ::= simple_expression

                      | complex_ expression

simple_expression   ::= event_name

                      | event_function

complex_expression ::= simple_expression boolean_operator

                        complex_expression

                      | simple_expression

boolean_operator    ::= ";" | "|" | "NOT"

event_function      ::= interval_function

                      | any_function

                      | anynew_function

                      | seq_function

                      | times_function

                      | in_function

interval_function ::= event_name ":" number ":"

                      event_name

any_function        ::= "ANY" "(" number ";" event_seq ")"
```

```
anynew_function   ::= "ANYNEW" "(" number ";"
                           event_seq ")"

seq_function      ::= "SEQ" "(" event_seq ")"

times_function    ::= "TIMES" "(" number ";" event_seq ")"

in_function       ::= "IN" "(" event_name ";" interval ")"

event_seq         ::= event_name ( ";" event_name )*

interval          ::= number ";" positive_number
                       |  season ";" season

season       ::= "WINTER"  |  "SPRING"  |  "SUMMER"  |  "AUTUMN"
```

##

```
instruction_stream ::= special_actor_name actor_operator
                        ( number actor_name actor_operator )*
                        | actor_name(actor_operator
                        actor_name)+

special_actor_name ::= "$"  |  actor_name

actor_operator     ::= ">"  |  "!"  |  "||"  |  "|>"  |  "/\"
```

##

```
positive_number ::= positive_digit ( number | e )*

number          ::= digit
                    |  digit number

string          ::= character
                    |  character string

character       ::= lower_case_char
                    |  upper_case_char
```

```
                    |  digit

                    |  special_char

lower_case_char ::= "a"  |  "b"  |  "c"  |  "d"  |  "e"  |  "f"  |

                    "g"  |  "h"  |  "i"  |  "j"  |  "k"  |  "l"  |
                    "m"  |  "n"  |  "o"  |  "p"  |  "q"  |  "r"  |

                    "s"  |  "t"  |  "u"  |  "v"  |  "w"  |  "x"  |
                    "y"  |  "z"


upper_case_char ::= "A"  |  "B"  |  "C"  |  "D"  |  "E"  |  "F"  |

                    "G"  |  "H"  |  "I"  |  "J"  |  "K"  |  "L"  |

                    "M"  |  "N"  |  "O"  |  "P"  |  "Q"  |  "R"  |

                    "S"  "T"  |  "U"  |  "V"  |  "W"  |  "X"  |

                    "Y"  |  "Z"

digit             ::= positive_digit  |  "0"

positive_digit  ::= "1"  |  "2"  |  "3"  |  "4"  |  "5"  |  "6"  |
"7"

                    |  "8"  |  "9"

special_char    ::= "."  |  ":"  |  "/"  |  "\"
```

Note

For the above notation we have:

- the symbol "*" means repeat zero or more times

- the symbol "*" means repeat one or more times

- the symbol "e" represents the empty word

References

[A83] J.F. Allen: "Maintaining Knowledge about Temporal Intervals". Communications of the ACM, Vol. 26, No. 11, November 1983, pp. 832-843.

[All83] J.F.Allen. "Maintaining Knowledge about Temporal Intervals". Communications of the ACM, 26(11), November 1983.

[Beck90] N. Beckmann, H.-P. Kriegel, R. Schneider, B. Seeger, "The R*-tree: An Efficient and Robust Access Method for Points and Rectangles", Proceedings of ACM SIGMOD International Conference on Management of Data, 1990.

[Bent75] J.L. Bentley, "Multidimensional Binary Search Trees Used for Associative Searching", Communications of the ACM, vol. 18, pp. 509-517, 1975.

[BKL96] S. Boll, W. Klas, M. Löhr. "Integrated Database Services for Multimedia Presentations". In S.M. Chung (editor), Multimedia Information Storage and Management, to be published by Kluwer Academic Publishers, 1996.

[Brin93] T. Brinkhoff, H.-P. Kriegel, B. Seeger, "Efficient Processing of Spatial Joins using R-trees", Proceedings of ACM SIGMOD International Conference on Management of Data, 1993.

[BS96] G. Blakowski, R. Steinmetz, "A Media Synchronization Survey: Reference Model, Specification, and Case Studies", IEEE Journal on Selected Areas in Communications, vol 14, No. 1, Jan. 1996, pp. 5-35.

[BZ95] Buchanan M.C., Zellweger P.T., "Automatically generating consistent schedules for multimedia documents", *ACM-Multimedia Systems Journal*, vol. 1 (2), pp. 55-67.

[Chiu94] T. Chiueh, "Content-Based Image Indexing", Proceedings of the 20th International Conference on Very Large Databases (VLDB), 1994.

[CM89] S. Chakravarthy, D. Mishra. Rule management and evaluation: an active DBMS prospective.In[S89].

[CM93] S. Chakravarthy, D. Mishra. "Snoop: An Expressive Event Specification Language For Active Databases". Technical Report, UF-CIS-TR-93-00, University of Florida, 1993.

[CO96] Courtiat J.P., De Oliveira R.C., "Proving Temporal Consistency in a New Multimedia Synchronization Model,", in the Proceedings of ACM Multimedia 1996 Conference.

[Falo94] C. Faloutsos, W. Equitz, M. Flickner, W. Niblack, D. Petkovic, R. Barber, "Efficient and Effective Querying by Image Content", Journal of Intelligent Information Systems, vol. 3, pp. 1-28, July 1994.

[G94] S. Gatziou. "Events in Active Object-Oriented Database System". Technical Report, ETH, Zurich, 1994.

156   References

[GJS92]   N.H. Gehani, H.V. Jagadish, O. Shmueli, "Event Specification in an
            Active Object Oriented Database", In Proceedings of the
            ACM/SIGMOD Conference, 1992.

[Gutt84]   A. Guttman, "R-trees: A Dynamic Index Structure for Spatial
            Searching", Proceedings of ACM SIGMOD International Conference
            on Management of Data, 1984.

[H92]   P. Hoepner, "Synchronizing the Presentation of Multimedia Objects",
            Computer Communications, Vol. 15, No. 9, November 1992, pp. 557-
            564.

[H96]   M. Handl, "A New Multimedia Synchronization model", IEEE Journal
            on Selected Areas in Communications, vol 14, No. 1, Jan. 1996, pp. 73-
            83.

[HFK95]   N. Hirzalla, B. Falchuk, A. Karmouch. „A Temporal Model for
            Interactive Multimedia Scenarios", IEEE Multimedia, Fall 1995, pp.
            24-31.

[IDG94]   M. Iino, Y.F. Day, A. Ghafoor. "An Object Oriented Model for
            Spatiotemporal Synchronization of Multimedia Information". In Proc.
            IEEE Int. Conf. Multimedia Computing and Systems, Boston MA,
            1994, pp. 110-119.

[Iin94]   M. Iino, Y. F. Day, A. Ghafoor, "An Object - Oriented Model for
            Spatiotemporal Synchronization of Multimedia Information", in the
            proc. of the IEEE Multimedia Conference, 1994, pp. 110-119.

[ISO92]   International Standard Organization. "Hypermedia/Time-based
            Document Structuring Language (HyTime)", ISO/IEC IS 10744, April
            1992.

[ISO93]   ISO/IEC. JTC 1/SC 29, "Coded Representation of Multimedia and
            Hypermedia Information Objects (MHEG)", Part I, Committee Draft
            13522-1, June 1993. ISO/IEC 10031.

[J97a]   Java-Remote Method Invocation, available at:
            http://java.sun.com:81/marketing/collateral/rmi_ds.html

[J97b]   Java–Media Framework, available at:
            http://www.javasoft.com/products/java-media/jmf/

[KE96]   Karmouch. A, Emery J., "A playback Schedule Model for Multimedia
            Documents", IEEE Multimedia, v3(1), pp. 50-63, 1996

[Koe93]   Koegel, J.F., Rutledge, L.W, Rutledge, J.L, and Keskin, C. Hyoctane:
            A HyTime Engine for and MMIS. In Proc. ACM Multimedia 93, pages
            129-136, Anaheim, CA, August 1993.

[Kolo91]   C.P. Kolovson, M. Stonebraker, "Segment Indexes: Dynamic Indexing
            Techniques for Multi-Dimensional Interval Data", Proceedings of
            ACM SIGMOD International Conference on Management of Data,
            1991.

[Krie96]   Peter Krieg, "Digital Hollywood The turbulent Marraige of Computer,
            Telecom and Media Industry", in the proceedings of International
            Workshop on Multimedia Software Development (MMSD), 1996

[LG93]   T. Little, A. Ghafoor. "Interval-Based Conceptual Models for Time-
            Dependent Multimedia Data, IEEE Transactions on Data and
            Knowledge Engineering, Vol. 5, No. 4, August 93, pp. 551-563.

[LK95]   N. Layaida and C. Keramane, "Maintaining Temporal Consistency of Multimedia Documents", Proceedings of the ACM Workshop on Effective Abstractions in Multimedia, San Francisco, November 1995.

[Oren86]   J. Orenstein, "Spatial Query Processing in an Object-Oriented Database System", Proceedings of ACM SIGMOD International Conference on Management of Data, 1986.

[Page93]   B.-U. Pagel, H.-W. Six, H. Toben, P. Widmayer, "Towards an Analysis of Range Query Performance", Proceedings of the 12th ACM Symposium on Principles of Database Systems (PODS), 1993.

[Papa95]   D. Papadias, Y. Theodoridis, T. Sellis, M. Egenhofer, "Topological Relations in the World of Minimum Bounding Rectangles: a Study with R-trees", Proceedings of ACM SIGMOD International Conference on Management of Data, 1995.

[PR94]   B. Prabhakaran and S.V. Raghavan (1994) { Synchronization Models for Multimedia Presentation With User Participation}, ACM/Springer-Verlag Journal of Multimedia Systems, vol.2, no. 2, August 1994, pp. 53-62.

[S89]   Sellis, T. Editor.Special issue on rule management and processing in expert database systems. SIGMOD Record (18) 3 (1989).

[Same90]   H. Samet, "The Design and Analysis of Spatial Data Structures", Addison-Wesley, 1990.

[Sell87]   T. Sellis, N. Roussopoulos, C. Faloutsos, "The R+-tree: A Dynamic Index for Multidimensional Objects", Proceedings of the 13th International Conference on Very Large Databases (VLDB), 1987.

[SKD96]   J. Schnepf, A. Kosntan, D.H. Du. "Doing FLIPS: FLexible Interactive Presentation Synchronisation", IEEE Journal on Selected Areas in Communications, Vol. 14, No . 1, January 1996, pp. 114-125.

[SMI98]   Synchronized Multimedia Integration Language, W3C Working Draft 2-February-98, available at: http://www.w3.org/TR/WD-smil/

[SW95]   G. Schloss, M. Wynblatt. "Providing definition and temporal structure from multimedia data", Multimedia Systems Journal, Vol. 3, 1995, pp. 264-277.

[Theo96a]   Y. Theodoridis, M. Vazirgiannis, T. Sellis, "SpatioTemporal Indexing for Large Multimedia Applications", Proceedings of the 3rd IEEE Conference on Multimedia Computing and Systems (ICMCS), 1996.

[Theo96b]   Y. Theodoridis, T. Sellis, "A Model for the Prediction of R-tree Performance", Proceedings of the 15th ACM Symposium on Principles of Database Systems (PODS), 1996.

[TKWPC96]   H. Thimm, Wolfgang Klas, Jonathan Walpole, Calton Pu, Crispin Cowan. "Managing Adaptive Presentation Executions in Distributed Multimedia Database Systems". In: Proceedings of International Workshop on Multimedia Database Systems, Blue Mountain Lake, NY, 1995.

[Ubel94]   "The Montage Extensible Datablade Architecture", Proc. ACM SIGMOD Conference, May 1994.

[V96]   M. Vazirgiannis, "Multimedia Data Base Object and Application Modelling Issues and an Object Oriented Model" in the book "Multimedia Database Systems: Design and Implementation Strategies" (editors Kingsley C. Nwosu, Bhavani Thuraisingham and P. Bruce Berra), Kluwer Academic Publishers, 1996, Pages: 208-250

[Vaz98]   M. Vazirgiannis, Y. Theodoridis, T. Sellis, "Spatiotemporal Composition and Indexing for Large Multimedia Applications", to appear in ACM/Springer-Verlag Multimedia Systems Journal, 1998.

[VB97]   M. Vazirgiannis, S. Boll, "Events In Interactive Multimedia Applications: Modeling And Implementation Design", in the proceedings of IEEE International Conference on Multimedia Computing and Systems (ICMCS'97), June 1997, Ottawa, Canada.

[VM93]   M. Vazirgiannis, C. Mourlas, "An object Oriented Model for Interactive Multimedia Applications", The Computer Journal, British Computer Society, vol. 36(1), 1/1993.

[VS96]   M. Vazirgiannis, T. Sellis. "Event and Action Representation and Composition for Multimedia Application Scenario Modelling". In the procedings of ERCIM Workshop on Interactive Distributed Multimedia Systems and Services, BERLIN, 3/1996.

[VTS96]   M. Vazirgiannis, Y. Theodoridis, T. Sellis. "Spatio Temporal Composition in Multimedia Applications". In: Proceedings of the IEEE - ICSE '96 International Workshop on Multimedia Software Development - BERLIN, 3/1996.

[VTS98]   M. Vazirgiannis, Y. Theodoridis, T. Sellis, "Spatiotemporal Composition and Indexing for Large Multimedia Applications" , to appear in ACM/Springer-Verlag Multimedia Systems Journal, 1997

Subject Index

Lecture Notes in Computer Science

For information about Vols. 1–1650
please contact your bookseller or Springer-Verlag

Vol. 1689: F. Solina, A. Leonardis (Eds.), Computer Analysis of Images and Patterns. Proceedings, 1999. XIV, 650 pages. 1999.

Vol. 1690: Y. Bertot, G. Dowek, A. Hirschowitz, C. Paulin, L. Théry (Eds.), Theorem Proving in Higher Order Logics. Proceedings, 1999. VIII, 359 pages. 1999.

Vol. 1691: J. Eder, I. Rozman, T. Welzer (Eds.), Advances in Databases and Information Systems. Proceedings, 1999. XIII, 383 pages. 1999.

Vol. 1692: V. Matoušek, P. Mautner, J. Ocelíková, P. Sojka (Eds.), Text, Speech and Dialogue. Proceedings, 1999. XI, 396 pages. 1999. (Subseries LNAI).

Vol. 1693: P. Jayanti (Ed.), Distributed Computing. Proceedings, 1999. X, 357 pages. 1999.

Vol. 1694: A. Cortesi, G. Filé (Eds.), Static Analysis. Proceedings, 1999. VIII, 357 pages. 1999.

Vol. 1695: P. Barahona, J.J. Alferes (Eds.), Progress in Artificial Intelligence. Proceedings, 1999. XI, 385 pages. 1999. (Subseries LNAI).

Vol. 1696: S. Abiteboul, A.-M. Vercoustre (Eds.), Research and Advanced Technology for Digital Libraries. Proceedings, 1999. XII, 497 pages. 1999.

Vol. 1697: J. Dongarra, E. Luque, T. Margalef (Eds.), Recent Advances in Parallel Virtual Machine and Message Passing Interface. Proceedings, 1999. XVII, 551 pages. 1999.

Vol. 1698: M. Felici, K. Kanoun, A. Pasquini (Eds.), Computer Safety, Reliability and Security. Proceedings, 1999. XVIII, 482 pages. 1999.

Vol. 1699: S. Albayrak (Ed.), Intelligent Agents for Telecommunication Applications. Proceedings, 1999. IX, 191 pages. 1999. (Subseries LNAI).

Vol. 1700: R. Stadler, B. Stiller (Eds.), Active Technologies for Network and Service Management. Proceedings, 1999. XII, 299 pages. 1999.

Vol. 1701: W. Burgard, T. Christaller, A.B. Cremers (Eds.), KI-99: Advances in Artificial Intelligence. Proceedings, 1999. XI, 311 pages. 1999. (Subseries LNAI).

Vol. 1702: G. Nadathur (Ed.), Principles and Practice of Declarative Programming. Proceedings, 1999. X, 434 pages. 1999.

Vol. 1703: L. Pierre, T. Kropf (Eds.), Correct Hardware Design and Verification Methods. Proceedings, 1999. XI, 366 pages. 1999.

Vol. 1704: Jan M. Żytkow, J. Rauch (Eds.), Principles of Data Mining and Knowledge Discovery. Proceedings, 1999. XIV, 593 pages. 1999. (Subseries LNAI).

Vol. 1705: H. Ganzinger, D. McAllester, A. Voronkov (Eds.), Logic for Programming and Automated Reasoning. Proceedings, 1999. XII, 397 pages. 1999. (Subseries LNAI).

Vol. 1706: J. Hatcliff, T. Æ. Mogensen, P. Thiemann (Eds.), Lectures on Partial Evaluation. Proceedings, 1998. IX, 433 pages. 1999. (Subseries LNAI).

Vol. 1707: H.-W. Gellersen (Ed.), Handheld and Ubiquitous Computing. Proceedings, 1999. XII, 390 pages. 1999.

Vol. 1708: J.M. Wing, J. Woodcock, J. Davies (Eds.), FM'99 – Formal Methods. Proceedings Vol. I, 1999. XVIII, 937 pages. 1999.

Vol. 1709: J.M. Wing, J. Woodcock, J. Davies (Eds.), FM'99 – Formal Methods. Proceedings Vol. II, 1999. XVIII, 937 pages. 1999.

Vol. 1710: E.-R. Olderog, B. Steffen (Eds.), Correct System Design. XIV, 417 pages. 1999.

Vol. 1711: N. Zhong, A. Skowron, S. Ohsuga (Eds.), New Directions in Rough Sets, Data Mining, and Granular-Soft Computing. Proceedings, 1999. XIV, 558 pages. 1999. (Subseries LNAI).

Vol. 1712: H. Boley, A Tight, Practical Integration of Relations and Functions. XI, 169 pages. 1999. (Subseries LNAI).

Vol. 1713: J. Jaffar (Ed.), Principles and Practice of Constraint Programming – CP'99. Proceedings, 1999. XII, 493 pages. 1999.

Vol. 1714: M.T. Pazienza (Eds.), Information Extraction. IX, 165 pages. 1999. (Subseries LNAI).

Vol. 1715: P. Perner, M. Petrou (Eds.), Machine Learning and Data Mining in Pattern Recognition. Proceedings, 1999. VIII, 217 pages. 1999. (Subseries LNAI).

Vol. 1716: K.Y. Lam, E. Okamoto, C. Xing (Eds.), Advances in Cryptology – ASIACRYPT'99. Proceedings, 1999. XI, 414 pages. 1999.

Vol. 1717: Ç. K. Koç, C. Paar (Eds.), Cryptographic Hardware and Embedded Systems. Proceedings, 1999. XI, 353 pages. 1999.

Vol. 1718: M. Diaz, P. Owezarski, P. Sénac (Eds.), Interactive Distributed Multimedia Systems and Telecommunication Services. Proceedings, 1999. XI, 386 pages. 1999.

Vol. 1719: M. Fossorier, H. Imai, S. Lin, A. Poli (Eds.), Applied Algebra, Algebraic Algorithms and Error-Correcting Codes. Proceedings, 1999. XIII, 510 pages. 1999.

Vol. 1721: S. Arikawa, K. Furukawa (Eds.), Discovery Science. Proceedings, 1999. XI, 374 pages. 1999. (Subseries LNAI).

Vol. 1722: A. Middeldorp, T. Sato (Eds.), Functional and Logic Programming. Proceedings, 1999. X, 369 pages. 1999.

Vol. 1723: R. France, B. Rumpe (Eds.), UML'99 – The Unified Modeling Language99. XVII, 724 pages. 1999.

Vol. 1726: V. Varadharajan, Y. Mu (Eds.), Information and Communication Security. Proceedings, 1999. XI, 325 pages. 1999.

Vol. 1727: P.P. Chen, D.W. Embley, J. Kouloumdjian, S.W. Liddle, J.F. Roddick (Eds.), Advances in Conceptual Modeling. Proceedings, 1999. XI, 389 pages. 1999.

Vol. 1728: J. Akoka, M. Bouzeghoub, I. Comyn-Wattiau, E. Métais (Eds.), Conceptual Modeling – ER '99. Proceedings, 1999. XIV, 540 pages. 1999.

Vol. 1729: M. Mambo, Y. Zheng (Eds.), Information Security. Proceedings, 1999. IX, 277 pages. 1999.

Vol. 1734: H. Hellwagner, A. Reinefeld (Eds.), SCI: Scalable Coherent Interface. XXI, 490 pages. 1999.

Vol. 1564: M. Vazirgiannis, Interactive Multimedia Documents. XIII, 161 pages. 1999.

Vol. 1591: D.J. Duke, I. Herman, S. Marshall, PREMO: A Framework for Multimedia Middleware. XII, 254 pages. 1999.